THE PERSON
WITH POWER

Holy Spirit Dwelling on the inside

By Teresa S. Mccurry

Copyright © 2019 by Teresa S. McCurry
All rights reserved. This book or any portion thereof may not be reproduced or used in any manner whatsoever without the express written permission of the publisher except for the use of brief quotations in a book review.

Printed in the United States of America

First Printing, 2019

ISBN 978-1-7338770-0-8 (sc)
ISBN 978-1-7338770-5-3 (e)

McCurry Ministries International
2060 West 65th Street
Cleveland, Ohio 44102
(216) 916-9270

www.MyNewBeginning.org

Contents

Foreword v
Introduction... vii
Chapter 1: Who Is The Holy Spirit? 1
Chapter 2: Holy Spirit Upon Believers............................. 15
Chapter 3: The Fruit Of The Spirit.................................... 28
Chapter 4: The Fruit Of The Holy Spirit........................... 45
Chapter 5: The Fruit Of The Spirit.................................... 59
Chapter 6: Cultivating Good Habits 71
Chapter 7: Breaking Generational Curses......................... 82
Chapter 8: The Gifts Of The Spirit 90
Chapter 9: The Gifts Of The Spirit 102
Chapter 10: The Gifts Of The Spirit 111
Chapter 11: "Blow The Trumpet In Zion" 129
Acknowledgments 142
About The Author 146
Invest In You !! 148
Follow Her On Social Media 149

Foreword

I consider it an honor to write this foreword.

The author shows her genuine love for and trust in the person of the Holy Spirit. The simplicity of her writing allows those who read this book to have better understanding of Who He is and His works in the life of the believer.

It is obvious she has spent time with her research to make sure the reader has valid information concerning the need for Him in his/her life.

I do recommend this book for new believers and those who were taught that His power and supernatural ability are not for this time

Apostle Winnie E. Hamilton PhD.

Apostle to the Nations, Son Rise Global Ministries

INTRODUCTION

In 2017 I preached a sermon series entitled The Person with POWER – The Holy Spirit, the Third Person. I had been studying the Holy Spirit for my own personal empowerment and I felt a strong leading of the Holy Spirit to teach the church what I had learned for myself. The response from our congregation was overwhelming ... the ladies in the media CD ministry told me each month the CDs were selling out and they had to make more copies each week. I was excited because that confirmed that the people were hungry for more teaching on the Holy Spirit.

> *How then shall they call on Him in whom they have not believed? And how shall they believe in Him of whom they have not heard? And how shall they hear without a preacher?* (Romans 10:14)

I believe the teaching inspires the people to have a better understanding of who the Holy Spirit is and how the Holy Spirit works. When we know how the Holy Spirit works in our lives, that's how we receive POWER. I'm excited that the Holy Spirit will work in the lives of the people who choose to read this book. I ask one thing of you and that is to be expectant of the miraculous things the Holy Spirit is going to do in your life.

At the same time I had to prioritize my responsibilities. My schedule is full most of the time ... I love to be productive. Please! Please don't call me A BUSY LADY! NO ... I am not busy *" like a dog chasing it tail, or like a hamster running around the wheel"* . I prefer to see myself as a very productive woman with the help of the resources that are around me.

So, once it was clear to me that this teaching should be put into a book, I had my sermons transcribed. The next step was to find the right content editor to help me with the process. My content editor was Fleur Vaz from Malaysia and I know the Holy Spirit led me to her. Reading her bio, I was very impressed by the simple fact that she is a Christian and wanted to help Christian writers. I ran across her bio at least six months before I reached out to her because I was gathering everything that I needed for the book. I know that God is going to use this book internationally, and the help that Fleur gave me was amazing. For this, I am forever grateful to God.

In this book I lay some key foundations based on the Person, role and operations of the Holy Spirit. How the Holy Spirit as the Third Person of the Godhead has always been with man since creation to NOW! How the Holy Spirit came upon believers in the Old Testament to empower them to do supernatural acts. How before Jesus ascended into heaven He promised to leave us a Helper the Holy Spirit, who has always led and guided believers. How He fell upon the disciples on the Day of Pentecost, who then turned the world upside down for Jesus.

At New Beginning Ministries (NBM) our services are led by the Holy Spirit. Yes there is an order of service but we are always ready for the Holy Spirit to have His way anytime during the service. Part of our vision statement states:

> "We Walk in the fruit of the Spirit, Operate in the gifts and Daily put on the whole armor of God, Believing in the fivefold ministry offices, and taking part in the evidence of His Glory with signs, wonder and Miracles
> ….
>
> WE LONG TO SEE LIVES TRANSFORMED BY INTRODUCING A REAL GOD, TO REAL PEOPLE WITH REAL ISSUES."

It was about five years ago when my husband and I discovered that God had given me the anointing to pray with and for people to receive the gifts of the Holy Spirit with the evidence of speaking in tongues ... as the Apostle Paul did: *"I thank my God I speak with tongues more than you all"* (1 Corinthians 14:18).

The Word of God teaches that, when we are filled with the Holy Ghost, we speak with other tongues as He gives utterance. This is the initial evidence, or sign, of the baptism of the Holy Spirit: *"And they were all FILLED WITH THE HOLY GHOST, and began to SPEAK WITH OTHER TONGUES, as the Spirit gave them utterance"* (Acts 2:4).

But the tongue can no man tame ... (James 3:8).

No man can tame the tongue because it is so unwieldy. Therefore, yielding our tongue to the Holy Spirit is a big step toward being able to fully yield all of our members to God. If you can yield your tongue, you can yield any part of your body to God.

And this is only the beginning of a supernatural life. God has much more to give those who are hungry. We, on our part, must be open to a fresh encounter with the Holy Spirit and not be boxed in by our personal belief systems, traditions, or complacency.

If you come from such a background and are skeptical about the power of the Holy Spirit, I want to encourage you by sharing this story.

One Sunday, while I was ministering the word of God, this young lady walks in during the end of my teaching ... she sits in the back of the church as I am concluding my message. The anointing for deliverance was in the house, so I laid hands on people and anointed them with oil. The lady visitor who had arrived – late by my standards (but for God she was right on time) – came to the altar with tears in her eyes, saying she wanted more of God. I asked her whether she was saved and she said, "Yes." I asked her whether she had the Holy Spirit with the evidence of speaking in tongues and she said, "No." I then asked her whether she wanted the gift, and she did. I explained to her that it was a gift from God and, if she believed, she would receive all she asked for. All she had to do was ask (see Luke 11:11-13).

Through her tears with hands lifted up, she nodded in agreement and repeated after me this simple prayer:

> "Lord, I ask that you fill me with your precious Holy Spirit with the evidence of speaking in tongues ... Just like the disciples in the upper room on the day of Pentecost, I will be filled with the Holy Spirit and begin to speak in tongues, as the Spirit gives me utterance."

I touched her belly and she began to speak ... her eyes got big and she started speaking louder. To her amazement, she started speaking in her heavenly language, stomping her feet, waving her hands and speaking in tongues! Praise God! Glory to his NAME!!

However, after that Sunday we did not see her for about a month. Deacon Reginald Walker had originally met Monica at the gas station and invited her to church ... was that a coincidence?? There's no such thing! God had divinely orchestrated their meeting. God knew all the time that she was going to be his wife, and that they were going to come together and work in ministry. We serve an AWESOME GOD!!

You see, about two years prior, Deacon Walker had received a word of prophesy that God was sending him a wife ... and he was instructed to set two plates at his dinner table every day because his wife was coming.

Fast forward. The lady, who we shall call Monica, was at the time attending another church that did not believe in the gifts of the Holy Spirit. Once she went back to her church, she knew that she could not use her gift there (she told me her life was changed that day and in her spirit she knew something was different). But they did not believe in speaking in tongues. Then, lo and behold, one day she was at a church prayer meeting with a group of ladies and, as they began to pray, she felt the gift of tongues bubbling up on the inside. "NO-NO-NO- NO, not now!" she thought as words in her heavenly language came forth.

Today, Monica is training in ministry and is married to Deacon Reggie Walker. They both serve the Lord faithfully in our ministry. Deacon Reggie had received from the Holy Spirit the Word of Knowledge and Word of Wisdom about the woman God was about to send to be his wife ... He had the choice to believe it and receive it, or reject it and neglect it. The two plates on the dinner table said it all!

Friend, it's all about faith. Salvation, healing, and the baptism in the Holy Ghost are all gifts that you receive by faith! You first receive that salvation, healing, and the baptism in the Holy Ghost in your spirit, or your heart. The bible says, *"With the heart man believes ..."* (Romans 10:10). Faith is of the heart. How does faith come? By hearing the Word of God (Romans 10:17).

When ministering the baptism in the Holy Spirit, I show people what the Word of God says about the experience. From Acts 2 through Acts 19, almost every time folks received the Holy Ghost, it says or infers that they spoke with tongues (see Acts 2:1–4; Acts 8:14–18; Acts 10:44–46; Acts 19:1–6). So when I minister to people, I make sure they expect to receive the baptism in the Holy Ghost with the evidence of speaking in tongues. Their expectation affects their receiving. I say, "I'm going to lay my hands on you. The Holy Ghost will come upon you. Your tongue will want to say something that isn't your native language: just speak it out."

The story of Monica and Reggie is one of the many testimonies of changed lives I will be sharing in the book. I have used speaking in tongues as an illustration of one of the gifts of the Holy Spirit. But, really, it is the start of the release of all the spiritual gifts bestowed by the Holy Spirit together with the grace gifts bestowed by the Father and the ministry gifts by Jesus.

We see all these gifts in operation in the days of the early church.

From that great event on the Day of Pentecost when the Holy Spirit fell on the 120 disciples of Jesus in tongues of fire, a revival broke out and multitudes of souls were continually added to the kingdom (see Acts 2). Signs and wonders followed the preaching of the word just as Jesus had commanded:

> *"Go into all the world and preach the gospel to every creature. He who believes and is baptized will be saved; but he who does not believe will be condemned. And these signs will follow those who believe: In My name they will cast out demons; they will speak with new tongues; they will take up serpents; and if they drink anything deadly, it will by no means hurt them; they will lay hands on the sick, and they will recover"* (Mark 16:15-18).

The Book of Acts is a testimony of what the Holy Spirit could do among ordinary men and women who believed. And, because they stepped out in faith, healings, prophesying, raising of the dead to life, deliverance and supernatural encounters became part of their ministry so that they were able to take the gospel from Jerusalem, to Samaria, to Asia Minor, to Africa and to Europe.

Yes, these demonstrations of the power of the Holy Spirit are all spectacular. But no less spectacular is the quiet character transformation that took place in lives that were yielded to the Holy Spirit's processing. Among the disciples, we see dramatic transformation of a frightened, illiterate, rap-tag group to leaders with great boldness, tenacity, courage, compassion, wisdom, and passion to win souls, equipped with all the Spirit-led strategies needed to take the gospel to the ends of the earth. We, too, as we present ourselves to God as broken-vessels ready to be used for His purposes, can be confident He will use us, too.

This is essentially a teaching book but also an empowering one. As you are set free by the truth, you will also know your destiny and be energized to run your race.

The book begins with the all important question: Who is the Holy Spirit? Is He a force? A wind? A dove? Or a Divine Person who has been with man since the beginning of creation and now wishes to dwell in you?

We then explore the nine fruit of the Holy Spirit which help us lead disciplined, purposeful and holy lives to be ready vessels to contain the great power to move in the supernatural. This power will be released as we study the gifts of the Holy Spirit and earnestly desire them, especially the gift of prophecy.

These are exciting times. What an amazing, awesome time to be alive and walk in the grace of God! What a privilege to arise as sons of God and be flooded with light! Only then can we combat the darkness of ignorance and new levels of sin that are becoming so blatant in our society. Together, you and I are going to arise and shine because we know our God and will do great exploits in His name. And, as you walk with the Holy Spirit and lead a fruitful and holy life empowered by Him, you, too, will write the book of your life in this dispensation of grace. You, too, will have a story to tell.

So, my dear brother, my dear sister, as you go through this book, I pray that the spirit of wisdom and revelation may come upon you, and the eyes of your understanding will be enlightened so that you may know the hope of His calling, the richness of your inheritance in Christ, and the exceeding greatness of His power towards us who believe.

Chapter 1

WHO IS THE HOLY SPIRIT?

Jesus' Promise

On the night before He was crucified, Jesus was in the garden of Gethsemane with His disciples. It was a time of great sorrow and anxiety because in a short while He was going to depart from them. But Jesus begins to comfort them. He talks about the Holy Spirit, the Person who would come and dwell in them. This is the *Parakletos,* our Comforter, Helper, Advocate, the One who walks alongside us. Jesus assures the disciples that He would not leave them orphans. How could this be when He was leaving them physically? Because of the Parakletos who would be their link with Jesus at all times even when He went to heaven. This meant they would never be alone.

> *"And I will pray the Father, and He will give you another Helper, that He may abide with you forever – the Spirit of truth, whom the world cannot receive, because it neither sees Him nor knows Him; but you know Him, for He dwells with you and will be in you. I will not leave you orphans; I will come to you"* (John 14:16-17).

Jesus indeed went to the cross. He died and rose again after three days and is now seated in heavenly places with the Father. But we have not been abandoned because we have access to the Holy Spirit who is that vital connection between us and God. In the human heart there is always that longing to reach God. How is that possible? Listen again to Jesus ...

> *"But I tell you the truth, it is to your advantage that I go away; for if I do not go away, the Helper (Comforter, Advocate, Intercessor – Counselor, Strengthener, Standby) will not come to you; but if I go, I will send Him (the Holy Spirit) to you [to be in close fellowship with you]"* (John 16:7 AMP).

The key is to get to know the Third Person the Holy Spirit. Then can we know God's plan and direction as we go through life, from reading the Bible to making important decisions. When we learn more about Him, we will know that He has many valuable things to impart to us and we will yearn for more.

But, first, we need to know the truth about the Third Person the Holy Spirit In the midst of all the theories floating around about Him. So let us separate fact from fiction and learn about who He really is from the Bible. We will first look at His identity, then His personality and lastly His function in our lives.

Identity: Is the Holy Spirit a force?

Those who conform to the world understand there are energy forces in every living being such as *chi* in Chinese or *prana* in Hindu philosophy, and they may liken the Holy Spirit to one of these forces. It's true that the Holy Spirit manifests in many forms: a dove, a mighty rushing wind, tongues of fire. So is He a force? What does the Bible say about His identity? Simply put, the Bible declares that the Holy Spirit is a divine Person: He is God: the Third Person.

Let's look further into this. First, every pronoun reference to the Holy Spirit in the New Testament uses "he" not "it." In the original Greek language of the New Testament, the word for "spirit," *pneuma*, is neuter and, grammatically, it would normally take a neuter pronoun to be in agreement. Yet, in many cases, the pronoun linked with *pneuma* is not neuter but masculine (see John 15:26; 16:13-14). There is no other way to interpret the use of the "he" pronoun in relation to the Holy Spirit except that He is a personal being rather than an impersonal force.

The second indisputable fact is that the Holy Spirit is God. This is clearly seen in many scriptures. For instance, Matthew 28:19 teaches us to baptize in the name of the Father, Son, and Holy Spirit. This is a collective reference to the one Triune God: the Father, the Son and the Holy Spirit, the Third Person. In fact, at the beginning of Jesus' ministry we have a beautiful picture of the Trinity working together at the baptism of Jesus by John the Baptist:

> *When He had been baptized, Jesus came up immediately from the water; and behold, the heavens were opened to Him, and He saw the Spirit of God descending like a dove and alighting upon Him. And suddenly a voice came from heaven, saying, "This is My beloved Son, in whom I am well pleased"* (Matthew 3:16-17).

The centerpiece is Jesus submitting to the will of the Father to be baptized (though He was without sin), the Holy Spirit descending upon Him in the form of a dove, and the voice of the Father from heaven, endorsing the ministry of His beloved Son.

Again, in the book of Acts we see Peter confronting Ananias, who had lied about the sale of his land: *"Ananias, how is it that Satan has so filled your heart that you have lied to the Holy Spirit ... You have not lied just to human beings but to God"* (Acts 5:3-4 NIV). This is a clear declaration that lying to the Holy Spirit amounts to lying to God.

The Holy Spirit is God because He possesses three essential characteristics of God that no one else possesses. They are: omnipresence – the quality of being everywhere; omniscience – the ability to know all things; and eternality – eternality is more than immortality because it signifies without beginning or end.

The Holy Spirit's omnipresence is vividly expressed by David in Psalm 139:7-8:

> *"Where can I go from your Spirit? Where can I flee from your presence? If I go up to the heavens, you are there; if I make my bed in the depths, you are there"* (NIV).

Then we see the characteristic of omniscience:

> *But God has revealed them to us through His Spirit. For the Spirit searches all things, yes, the deep things of God. For what man knows the things of a man except the spirit of the man which is in him? Even so no one knows the things of God except the Spirit of God* (1 Corinthians 2:10-11).

Finally, the Holy Spirit is eternal as stated in the Books of Hebrews:

> *… how much more shall the blood of Christ, who through the **eternal Spirit** offered Himself without spot to God, cleanse your conscience from dead works to serve the living God?* (Hebrews 9:14)

Only a Being who is part of the Triune Godhead and possesses the attributes of omniscience, omnipresence, and eternality could be defined as God.

The personhood of the Holy Spirit is further affirmed by His many works. In the Book of Genesis we see Him personally involved in creation:

> *In the beginning **God** [Elohim] created the heavens and the earth. The earth was without form, and void; and darkness was on the face of the deep. And the **Spirit of God** was hovering over the face of the waters* (Genesis 1:1-2, emphasis added).

Here we see the Spirit of God, the Holy Spirit hovering over the face of the water, participating in the act of creation. It is also important to observe that the Hebrew name for God used here, *Elohim*, is used in the plural form, implying that all three Persons in the Trinity were collaborating in the work of creation.

Furthermore, the Holy Spirit empowers God's people (see Zechariah 4:6), He guides (see Romans 8:14), He comforts (see John 14:26), He convicts (see John 16:8), He teaches (see John 16:13), He restrains sin (see Isaiah 59:19), and He gives commands (see Acts 8:29). Each of these works requires the involvement of a person rather than a mere force, thing or idea.

Personality: Mind, Will and Emotions

As a divine Person, the Holy Spirit has a mind, emotions and a will like us. He thinks, knows and imparts knowledge to us:

> *But God has revealed them to us through His Spirit. For the Spirit searches all things, yes, the deep things of God. For what man knows the things of a man except the spirit of the man which is in him? Even so no one knows the things of God except the Spirit of God* (1 Corinthians 2:10-11).

He makes decisions according to His will:

> *But one and the same Spirit works all these things, distributing to each one individually **as He wills*** (1 Corinthians 12:11, emphasis added).

He searches our hearts and intercedes for us according to the will of God:

> *Now He who searches the hearts knows what the mind of the Spirit is, because He makes intercession for the saints according to the will of God* (Romans 8:27).

In addition, the Holy Spirit has emotions. He always brings joy and peace. But He can also be grieved. When calling upon the Ephesians to put away bitterness, wrath, anger, clamor, and evil speaking, Paul pleads with them: "*And do not grieve the Holy Spirit of God, by whom you were sealed for the day of redemption*" (Ephesians 4:30).

Scripture therefore makes it abundantly clear that the Holy Spirit is God and serves in perfect unity with Father and Son. He is therefore to be revered as God.

Functions of the Holy Spirit

When Jesus was describing the Holy Spirit to His disciples at Gethsemane, He named three of His main functions:

- Comforts and helps
- Teaches and leads into all truth
- Convicts and leads into righteousness

Comforts and Helps

The Parakletos, who Jesus promised, is the One who comforts and helps us through all of life's uncertainties. He is our Guide, our Teacher and Counselor, our Friend (see John 14:26). We can trade our restless thoughts for a sense of stability, peace and joy in every situation, knowing that we have a Friend who is utterly trustworthy, consistent and reliable.

We see throughout the Book of Acts how new believers filled with the Holy Spirit experienced great joy and peace. They could also see the amazing transformation of Saul from being an overzealous persecutor of new Christians to a fervent preacher of the gospel of Jesus Christ. His messages inspired peace in the hearts of the believers in Judea, Galilee, and Samaria. And the church grew.

> *So the church throughout all Judea and Galilee and Samaria enjoyed peace, being built up; and going on in the fear of the Lord and in the comfort of the Holy Spirit, it continued to increase* (Acts 9:31 NIV).

The Spirit, in His mighty power, continues to fill believers with *"all joy and peace"* as we trust the Lord, causing us to *"overflow with hope"* (See Romans 15:13). He continues to inspire men and women to release words of comfort and peace to one another – believers and non believers alike – touching lives.

And, even in the midst of trials, the Spirit comforts believers with His joy. Paul exhorts the people of Thessalonica to be joyful in the midst of affliction with these words: *"And you became followers of us and of the Lord, having received the word in much affliction, with joy of the Holy Spirit"* (1 Thessalonians 1:6).

We do not have to wait till we die to experience heaven. With the Holy Spirit, we can experience it now, for the Kingdom of God is *"righteousness and peace and joy in the Holy Spirit"* (Romans 14:17). It's a state of mind rather than a place. Some of the ways we can live in that Kingdom reality are when we choose to

- Abide in His presence

  David, repenting of his sin, pleads with the Lord, not to take the Holy Spirit away from him: *"Do not cast me away from Your presence, And do not take Your Holy Spirit from me"* (Psalm 51:11).

  We, too, can abide in His presence throughout the day, occasionally tuning into the mind of God in the midst of a busy day, praying and singing in our hearts in the Spirit. He will energize us. He will help us through our day-to-day challenges. He will sustain us in our stressful moments with His peace.

- Abide with Him in prayer

  The Holy Spirit assists us as we pray. He helps us build ourselves in our faith by praying in the Spirit (see Jude 1:20). Often we do not know how to pray in a particular situation because we have exhausted all our human strategies for prayer. When we turn to Him and ask Him to pray through us, the Bible says He will help us in our weaknesses and make intercession for us. Only He understands the things of the spirit realm: what battles need to be fought and how the battles will be waged. So we pray in tongues and that prayer has great power to bring about change.

> *Likewise the Spirit also helps in our weaknesses. For we do not know what we should pray for as we ought, but the Spirit Himself makes intercession for us with groanings which cannot be uttered. Now He who searches the hearts knows what the mind of the Spirit is, because He makes intercession for the saints according to the will of God* (Romans 8:26-27).

- Abide in the Word, which is the Bible. We shall discuss this in the next section.

Teaches and Leads into all Truth

In the Garden, Jesus tells us more about the Holy Spirit when He comes to us.

> *"But the Helper, the Holy Spirit, whom the Father will send in My name, He will teach you all things, and bring to your remembrance all things that I said to you"* (John 14:26).

> *"However, when He, the Spirit of truth, has come, He will guide you into all truth; for He will not speak on His own authority, but whatever He hears He will speak; and He will tell you things to come"* (John 16:13).

As our Teacher, the Holy Spirit will primarily give us greater revelation in the word. This is only logical since it is He who inspired the different writers of the Bible. Consider the fact that the Bible consists of 66 books written over 1500 years by more than 35 authors with vastly different personalities and different cultures spread over three continents, and presented in three different languages. Isn't it astounding that such diversity could still have bring out such great unity in the Spirit!

How could such unity be possible? Because they all point to one ultimate Author the Holy Spirit, who inspired and orchestrated this grand symphony. The Bible says:

> *All Scripture is given by inspiration of God, and is profitable for doctrine, for reproof, for correction, for instruction in righteousness, that the man of God may be complete, thoroughly equipped for every good work* (2 Timothy 3:16-17).

Note especially that the word "*inspiration*" comes from the Greek word *theopneustos*, which literally means "God breathed." Just as the Creator *Elohim* breathed life into the nostrils of the first man, so is the Holy Spirit breathing inspiration into the minds of the people He moved to write the Bible.

The Holy Spirit does not inspire further Scripture but He continues to give us fresh revelation into the word for specific occasions. All the scriptures aim at revealing the ways of God and His heart for His people and they give Him glory. This echoes the words of Jesus, *"He will glorify and honor Me, because He (the Holy Spirit) will take from what is Mine and will disclose it to you"* (John 16:14 AMP).

The Holy Spirit has laid out His grand narrative, the *logos*, the written and general word, in the Bible. And, as we read the written word seeking the Lord for answers to our questions, He will give us specific insight into each situation and season. This specific insight is known as the *rhema* word, the word God speaks to our hearts. Jesus told us "… *the [rhema] words that I have **spoken to you are spirit***

and are life" (John 6:63, emphasis added) and they apply to our here and now. They are saturated with the Holy Spirit, who brings life and healing in the particular situation in which they are applied.

I would like to add a word of caution. No matter how private the insights we have been given, they will never contradict the general word of God and be open to anything contrary. They must always be tested against the *logos* word "*... for prophecy never came by the will of man, but holy men of God spoke as they were moved by the Holy Spirit*" (2 Peter 1:21).

That is why it is so vital that we read the Bible every day. Then we can intimately know God's ways and His will for us at all times. Such a depth of understanding gives us wisdom by which we can know the mind of God. "*But God has revealed them to us through His Spirit. For the Spirit searches all things, yes, the deep things of God. For what man knows the things of a man except the spirit of the man which is in him? Even so no one knows the things of God except the Spirit of God*" (1 Corinthians 2:10–11). Since we have been given this amazing gift of God's Spirit inside ourselves, we can comprehend the thoughts of God, as revealed in the Scripture. This is wisdom from on high, rather than wisdom from man.

We are told in the book of Proverbs that wisdom is the principal thing. When we have wisdom, we have the promise of happiness, prosperity, long life, honor and peace (see Proverbs 3:13-18). Without wisdom, the Bible says we will be like beasts that perish (see Proverbs 49:20).

Brings Conviction and Sanctification

Jesus continues His discourse on the Holy Spirit:

> "*And He, when He comes, will convict the world about [the guilt of] sin [and the need for a Savior], and about righteousness, and about judgment: about sin [and the true nature of it], because they do not believe in Me [and*

> *My message]; about righteousness [personal integrity and godly character], because I am going to My Father and you will no longer see Me; about judgment [the certainty of it], because the ruler of this world (Satan) has been judged and condemned"* (John 16:8-11 AMP).

This scripture is addressed primarily at unbelievers who are characterized as *"the world."* Through the stirring of the Holy Spirit, unbelievers will realize they have sinned against a holy God and they will want to come to God. They will want to be in right relationship with God and be close to Him. They will also realize the consequences (judgment) if they remain in their sin and refuse to repent. But only the Holy Spirit can do this deep work of conviction, not man, for *"… no one can say that Jesus is Lord except through the Holy Spirit"* (1 Corinthians 12:3).

That is why it is pointless nagging someone to accept Jesus. That would only turn them off. Once we have shared the gospel to them through the word and in our own lives, we can only pray for and encourage them. Let the Holy Spirit continue speaking to them in their quiet moments.

We all love that powerful song "Amazing Grace." But how many of us know that is was written by John Newton an 18th century slave trader who used to sail with cargoes of slaves from the west coast of Africa to Dover, England? Newton had been raised by a godly mother. But after his mother died, he turned against God and led many sailors to reject the gospel. He used such profane language, he was known as "The Great Blasphemer."

On this particular voyage on March 21, 1748, they were caught is a devastating storm in the Atlantic and were in danger of sinking. As Newton struggled to navigate the ship, the words from Proverbs came to his mind and seemed to confirm his self-condemnation:

> *Because I have called, and ye refused; I have stretched out my hand, and no man regarded; but ye have set at*

nought all my counsel, and would none of my reproof: I also will laugh at your calamity; I will mock when your fear cometh; when your fear cometh as desolation, and your destruction cometh as a whirlwind; when distress and anguish cometh upon you. Then shall they call upon me, but I will not answer; they shall seek me early, but they shall not find me (Proverbs 1:24-28 KJV).

At this point Newton began to cry out to Jesus to save him. Finding a New Testament, he began to read Luke 11:13 KJV: "*If ye then, being evil, know how to give good gifts unto your children: how much more shall your heavenly Father give the Holy Spirit to them that ask him.*"

And the goodness of God led him to repentance – and safety. He writes in his diary, "On that day the Lord sent from on high and delivered me out of deep waters." Only God's amazing grace could have taken such an ungodly, profane, slave-trading sailor and transform him into a child of God. Newton later became a committed Christian minister.

What about the believer? Does he, too, need to be convicted of sin? Yes, he does. Our walk with the Lord is an ongoing process of being changed from our old carnal self to our new identity in Christ. This is the process of sanctification or being set apart or holy for the Lord. This is by no means an automatic process but a process of yielding to the cleansing and pruning work of the Holy Spirit as He guides us. But we can make the first start by making up our mind to cut ourselves loose from our old fleshly desires. We must learn to hate sin the way God hates sin.

When we are born again as new believers in Christ, it is our spirit that is regenerated by the Spirit of God. But our mind and emotions are still carnal and need to be renewed. Galatians 5:19-21 gives us a graphic picture of the sins of the flesh, from sexual sin, to idolatry to anger and strife to drunkenness. The Bible makes it very clear that *"those who practice such things shall not inherit the kingdom of God"* (Galatians 5:21). To overcome our old desires and habits, we need to allow the fruit of the Holy Spirit as described in Galatians 5:23-24 to develop. Like any fruit in the natural, growing will take time. We cannot become holy by sheer will power but have to humble ourselves before Him and say we need help.

And He will. As we grow in our fruit, the Holy Spirit gives us the strength to rise above our fleshly nature and be molded into the character of God. These are the nine fruit that He sows and nurtures in us so that we have the power to overcome sin (see Galatians 5:23-24). As we develop the fruit of love, peace, joy, kindness, goodness and others, people will know that we have changed and are more like Christ. We are, in fact, changing from glory to glory.

> *"Now the Lord is the Spirit, and where the Spirit of the Lord is, there is freedom. And we all, who with unveiled faces contemplate the Lord's glory, are being transformed into his image with ever-increasing glory, which come from the Lord, who is the Spirit"* (2 Corinthians 3:17–18 NIV).

People will desire to have what we have and be attracted to Christ. I believe that our character is our most powerful witness of Jesus over and above signs, wonders and miracles.

He Changed Me

As I reflect on how God in the Third Person of the Holy Spirit has changed my life, I can say I am a totally different person from I used to be. EVERY DAY I am changing ... let my husband tell it. I was A GOOD GIRL ... in some way I was a good girl, but I was not a GOD GIRL!!! I had malice in my heart. I lied, stole and cheated ... and, if I am not careful, I know it can happen again.

I do understand to be converted you have to be a willing participant. God gave us free will. At any given time you can yield to the leading of the Holy Spirit or go with your own will. You and I can choose to allow the fruit of the Spirit to come into our hearts and make us over … or not… the choice is yours. I tell people you know what life is like living the way you've been living …why don't you look at life AFRESH!!!

Since a lot of people debate about who is filled with the Holy Spirit and who is not, I feel I need to lay more foundations about the Holy Spirit. So in the next chapter I will discuss the role of the Holy Spirit in the Old Testament compared with New Covenant believers. It's also important that we understand the difference between **being filled** with the Holy Spirit and **being baptized** with the Holy Spirit so that we will desire all He has to give.

Chapter 2

HOLY SPIRIT UPON BELIEVERS

In Chapter 1 we laid some key foundations about the Holy Spirit to understand who He is and what His main functions are. We agreed that He is God, the Third Person of the Triune God. Second, He is a Person with a mind, will and emotions like us, not a force. And, thirdly, we discussed His main functions: to comfort and help, to teach and to lead, convict of sin and to sanctify.

There is still a lot of debate as to whether you need to be baptized in the Holy Spirit to have the Holy Spirit dwelling in you. Then there are also questions about whether there is a difference between being filled and being empowered by the Holy Spirit. In this chapter I would like to explain the difference. A final topic I would like to discuss is the role of the Holy Spirit in the lives of Old Testament believers.

INDWELLING VS. EMPOWERING HOLY SPIRIT

"Indwelling" is the action by which the Holy Spirit takes up permanent residence in the body of a believer in Jesus Christ. "Empowering" is when He gives legal authority and power to a person to enable them to do something beyond their natural ability.

Let us look at both these principles in light of the endless debate between believers from Pentecostal/Charismatic backgrounds and believers from traditional churches about which believers are filled with the Holy Spirit and which ones are not.

Traditional believers cite the conversation between Jesus and the Pharisee Nicodemus, in which Nicodemus was asking Jesus about the "new birth."

> *Jesus answered and said to him, "Most assuredly, I say to you, unless one is born again, he cannot see the kingdom of God."*
>
> *Nicodemus said to Him, "How can a man be born when he is old? Can he enter a second time into his mother's womb and be born?"*
>
> *Jesus answered, "Most assuredly, I say to you, unless one is born of water and the Spirit, he cannot enter the kingdom of God. That which is born of the flesh is flesh, and that which is born of the Spirit is spirit. Do not marvel that I said to you, 'You must be born again.' The wind blows where it wishes, and you hear the sound of it, but cannot tell where it comes from and where it goes. So is everyone who is born of the Spirit"* (John 3:3-8).

Verses 5-8 establish the truth that, the moment you are born again, you have the Holy Spirit living in you.

Pentecostals, on the other hand, refer to the baptism that John the Baptist talked about concerning Jesus' ministry: "*I indeed baptize you with water unto repentance, but He who is coming after me is mightier than I, whose sandals I am not worthy to carry. He will baptize you with the Holy Spirit and fire*" (Matthew 3:11, emphasis added).

This reference to baptism and fire is when Jesus baptizes you with the Holy Spirit. Jesus also mentioned being "*endued with power from on high*" when He prepared His disciples for the coming of the Holy Spirit.

> *"Behold, I send the Promise of My Father upon you; but tarry in the city of Jerusalem until you are **endued with power** from on high*" (Luke 24:49, emphasis added).

This baptism of fire and power was fulfilled on the day of Pentecost when the Holy Spirit descended on the disciples in tongues of fire (see Acts 2:24). Pentecostals therefore claim that, unless we are moving in the gifts of the Holy Spirit with the evidence of speaking in tongues, we have not received the Holy Spirit.

Who is right? Both are – to a degree. Let me explain.

There is a difference between the **in-filling** (or **in-dwelling**) Holy Spirit and the **empowering** Holy Spirit for the New Testament Christian. Let's go back to the Luke 24:49 episode where the risen Christ was about to ascend to heaven. Jesus told the disciples to remain in Jerusalem and wait for the time they would be *"endued with power from on high."* Clearly this refers to the baptism of the Holy Spirit, an event also recorded in the book of Acts.

> *"But you shall receive **power** when the Holy Spirit has come upon you; and you shall be witnesses to Me in Jerusalem, and in all Judea and Samaria, and to the end of the earth"* (Acts 1:8, emphasis added).

Ten days after Jesus ascended into heaven, the 120 disciples were gathered in an upper room in Jerusalem, when the Holy Spirit descended on them:

> *When the Day of Pentecost had fully come, they were all with one accord in one place. And suddenly there came a sound from heaven, as of a rushing mighty wind, and it filled the whole house where they were sitting. Then there appeared to them divided tongues, as of fire, and one sat upon each of them. And they were all filled with the Holy Spirit and began to speak with other tongues, as the Spirit gave them utterance* (Acts 2:1-4).

The first evidence of being baptized with the Holy Spirit was speaking in tongues. These were special tongues that each foreigner understood in their own language, although these languages were unknown to the tongues-speakers. This was followed by an eloquent speech of Peter attesting to the fulfillment of scripture. The people marveled that these words were coming from an uneducated fisherman who spoke with such authority and boldness. That day 3,000 of them were saved. And, as each chapter of the book of Acts unfolds, we see the mighty working of the Holy Spirit with teaching, healing, prophecy and all the gifts fully displayed. Is this not a demonstration of the power of the Holy Spirit as prophesied by Jesus in Mark 16:17-18?

> *"And these signs will follow those who believe: In My name they will cast out demons; they will speak with new tongues ..."*

Do you see what the empowerment of the Holy Spirit is?

What then is the in-filling of the Holy Spirit? Let's look at the occasion the resurrected Christ appeared to His disciples as they gathered in a room:

> *Then, the same day at evening, being the first day of the week, when the doors were shut where the disciples were assembled, for fear of the Jews, Jesus came and stood in the midst, and said to them, "Peace be with you." When He had said this, He showed them His hands and His side. Then the disciples were glad when they saw the Lord.*
>
> *So Jesus said to them again, "Peace to you! As the Father has sent Me, I also send you." And when He had said this,* **He breathed on them, and said to them, "Receive the Holy Spirit.** *If you forgive the sins of any, they are forgiven them; if you retain the sins of any, they are retained"* (John 20:19-23, emphasis added).

I believe that this was the time that the disciples received their salvation. Prior to that they had only received the baptism of John.

The Holy Spirit was not yet given because Jesus was not yet glorified (see John 7:39). Now that the atonement and resurrection had been fulfilled, Jesus had made a way for them to be born again and receive the Holy Spirit. This fulfilled Jesus' words to Nicodemus, " ... *unless one is born of water* (the word of God, the risen Christ) *and the Spirit, he cannot enter the kingdom of God* (John 3:3, emphasis added). On this occasion, Jesus breathed on them the breath of eternal life and gave them the Holy Spirit, who was to dwell in them and flow out from them (see John 7:38-39). It was at this time that the disciples received the life of the Spirit. But it was not until Pentecost that they received the power of the Spirit.

When you receive Jesus as your personal Lord and Savior, you also receive the in-filling of the Holy Spirit. Jesus had mentioned to the disciples two separate experiences of the Holy Spirit by these words: "*He dwells **with** you and will be **in** you*" (John 14:17, emphasis added). "*He dwells with you*" or abides with you is in the present tense referring to their status before Christ went to the cross. On the other hand, "*... and will be **in** you*" points to a future time after His resurrection, and suggests a more intimate relationship. This relationship was established when Jesus breathed on them so that the Holy Spirit could come and dwell in them.

When we receive Jesus as our Lord and Savior, Jesus breathes on us, too, and gives us the Holy Spirit. Now the Holy Spirit has come to dwell in us permanently as our Comforter, Teacher, Counselor and Friend. But there is much more to come.

You need to take the second step of being baptized and empowered with the Holy Spirit, and experience your own day of Pentecost. When Jesus baptizes you with the Holy Spirit, you receive the fire that will empower you to do great works in the name of Jesus. It will also give you access to all the Holy Spirit's gifts. Then you can truly fulfill your call to be a disciple of Jesus and do great exploits in His name.

WHAT ROLE DID THE HOLY SPIRIT HAVE AMONG OLD TESTAMENT BELIEVERS?

The Holy Spirit has always been among men since Adam. He was busy shaping the destiny of God's chosen people throughout the Old Testament, convicting them of sin, drawing them into fellowship with God and teaching them His laws and ways. The Holy Spirit obviously had to regenerate them and lead them as He continues to do up till today. However, His work would take on a different character after Pentecost.

In general, there are two ways Old Testament believers could have experienced the Holy Spirit.

The Holy Spirit Dwelled with Certain People

There is still debate among scholars about whether Old Testament believers could have been in-dwelt or in-filled by the Holy Spirit like New Covenant believers. Certainly, prophets like Daniel, Isaiah, Jeremiah and even Joseph, among others, enjoyed the Lord's abiding presence, which looked as if the Spirit dwelled **within** them rather than with them.

For example, God instructed Moses to anoint Joshua as leader because this was "*a man in whom is the Spirit*" (Numbers 27:18). In the case of Joseph, Pharaoh marveled at such a man "*in whom is the Spirit of God*" (Genesis 41:38). King Nebuchadnezzar, too, recognized that in Daniel was "*the Spirit of the Holy God*" (Daniel 4:8). Again, in reference to Daniel, now an old man, the Queen told King Belshazzar of Babylon, "*There is a man in your kingdom in whom is the Spirit of the Holy God*" who could interpret the writing on the wall (Daniel 5:11).

It was also said of David, only a youth when the prophet Samuel anointed him King of Israel, that "*the Spirit of the Lord came upon David **from that day forward**"* (1 Samuel 16:13, emphasis added).

David was a man after God's own heart and his great intimacy with the Holy Spirit is so abundantly clear in the Psalms. That is, until we hear David crying out to God in Psalm 51:11 *"Do not cast me away from Your presence, And do not take Your Holy Spirit from me"* because of his sin with Bathsheba. This suggests that the Spirit of God could come and go depending on one's spiritual condition.

The question is, could there have been a type of in-dwelling or in-filling of the Holy Spirit in such people for an extended period? The Bible does not state this in specific terms. But then we remember Jesus' words to His disciples, *"He dwells **with** you and will be in you."* If that was true of the disciples before the atonement, it must also have been true of Old Testament believers, because Jesus had yet to be glorified. It would therefore be safe to say that the Holy Spirit dwelled **with** rather than **in** Old Testament believers in varying degrees of intimacy based on their faith and obedience to the word of God.

The Holy Spirit Empowered Certain People

In the Old Testament, every time the Spirit of the LORD came UPON a person, it was to give them a special enabling or empowerment. They were endued with SUPERNATURAL POWER to accomplish the task God had for them.

The prophets Isaiah, Ezekiel, Jeremiah, Daniel, among others, had detailed long-range vision. They foretold the return of the captives from Babylon, the coming of the Messiah, the new heart of flesh that God would give His people in the new covenant and, in our modern age, the rebirth of Israel as a nation, and the end-time events leading to the second coming of Jesus.

How did the empowerment take place? To illustrate, let's examine the empowerment in the lives of three people: Saul, Gideon and Elijah.

- Saul's missed opportunity

The prophet Samuel anointed Saul commander-in-chief over Israel and prophesied that the Spirit of the LORD would come upon him, and he would prophesy and be turned into another man (see 1 Samuel 10:1-6). When Saul was met by a group of prophets, *"then the Spirit of God came upon him, and he prophesied among them."* He was so changed that the people wondered what had come upon the son of Kish (1 Samuel 10:10-11).

In due time Samuel declared Saul King over Israel publicly (see 1 Samuel 10:24). But Saul acted foolishly and disobeyed the commandment of the Lord on two major occasions. For this, the kingdom was finally stripped from him and passed on to David: *"The LORD has torn the kingdom of Israel from you today, and has given it to a neighbor of yours, who is better than you"* (1 Samuel 15:28).

In the end, due to his disobedience, instead of the abiding presence of the Lord, Saul was visited by a distressing spirit (see 1 Samuel 16:14).

- Gideon's mighty men

Gideon was threshing wheat in the winepress for fear of the Midianites when the Angel of the Lord appeared to him, addressing him as a mighty man of valor (see Judges 6:12). The LORD assured him that He would be with them and they would defeat the Midianites as one man (see Judges 6:16). As the Midianites gathered force and encamped in the Valley of Jezreel, ***"the Spirit of the LORD came upon Gideon"*** (Judges 6:34, emphasis added). As he blew the trumpet, it rallied the Israelite tribes to come together.

As Gideon's faith grew, God was able to bring down the size of his army. Gideon's troops numbering 32,000 were too many for God lest Israel claimed the victory and failed to give Him the glory. So, in obedience to God, Gideon reduced them to 22,000. Again, in obedience, the remaining 10,000 were whittled down to just 300. Imagine 300 men pitched against 135,000 Midianite troops! (see Judges 7:2-8)

And God's battle plan was equally unique. The weapons given to each man were a horn, and a jar with a torch inside it. At about midnight, they surrounded the camp of the enemy soldiers. Then, in one accord, they all blew their horns and broke their jars, shouting: *"The **sword** of the Lord and of **Gideon**!"* (Judges 7:20, emphasis added). The enemy soldiers woke up in panic and fled but they were easily routed by Gideon's 300. It is clear that the Spirit of God upon Gideon changed this fearful man to the mighty man of valor that God could use to accomplish His plan.

- Elijah's extraordinary feat

    We read in 1 Kings 18:26 that *"**the hand of the Lord came upon Elijah**; and he girded up his loins and ran ahead of Ahab to the entrance of Jezreel"* (emphasis added). This was the culmination of an extraordinary day for the prophet Elijah. Earlier in the day he had a showdown with the false prophets at Mount Carmel: the 450 prophets of Baal and the 400 prophets of Asherah. Elijah challenged them to a trial by fire involving two bulls as sacrifice. Each party would call upon their god to send fire from heaven to consume the offering.

    The prophets of Ball called upon their god all day long, even cutting themselves with knives and lances to get his attention – but to no avail. Then it was Elijah's turn. He commanded that four pots of water be poured over the bull he had laid on the stone altar and into the trench surrounding the altar.

    Then at the time of the evening sacrifice, he cried out to God:

"Lord God of Abraham, Isaac, and Israel, let it be known this day that You are God in Israel and I am Your

*servant, and that I have done all these things **at Your word**. Hear me, O LORD, hear me, that this people may know that You are the LORD God, and that You have turned their hearts back to You again."*

Then the fire of the LORD fell and consumed the burnt sacrifice, and the wood and the stones and the dust, and it licked up the water that was in the trench. Now when all the people saw it, they fell on their faces; and they said, "The LORD, He is God! The LORD, He is God!" (1 Kings 18:36-39, emphasis added).

All 450 of the Baal prophets were summarily executed. At that time there was famine in the land because Elijah had declared there would be no rain for three years. This time Elijah went up the mountain and prayed for rain, and soon the sky became black with clouds. So King Ahab rode away to Jezreel as the heavy rain fell.

Instead of resting, Elijah, on the Lord's direction and in His strength, ran ahead of the king's chariot at least 16 miles to the entrance of Jezreel. This was humanly impossible. Only the Spirit of the Lord could have sustained him (See 1 Kings 18:40-46).

Saul, Gideon and Elijah are examples of the numerous Old Testament believers empowered by the Holy Spirit to accomplish a divine plan. Others included Samson, who had superhuman strength on many occasions when *"the Spirit of the Lord came mightily upon him"* (see Judges 14:6), Jacob, who had great discernment in multiplying the speckled flocks assigned to him (see Genesis 31:8), Moses, in allowing the Spirit of God to transfer his leadership to the 70 elders of Israel (see Numbers 11:17); Elijah, who allowed a double portion of his anointing to be transferred to his successor Elisha (see 2 Kings 2:10-11).

When the assignment was accomplished, the enabling would generally leave the person. This is in contrast to the Holy Spirit's current role of indwelling believers and abiding in them *"forever"* (John 14:16).

All the same, with all their limitations, look at the achievements of our forefathers through the Holy Spirit's enabling:

> *For the time would fail me to tell of Gideon and Barak and Samson and Jephthah, also of David and Samuel and the prophets: who through faith subdued kingdoms, worked righteousness, obtained promises, stopped the mouths of lions, quenched the violence of fire, escaped the edge of the sword, out of weakness were made strong, became valiant in battle, turned to flight the armies of the aliens. Women received their dead raised to life again.*
>
> *Others were tortured, not accepting deliverance, that they might obtain a better resurrection. Still others had trial of mockings and scourgings, yes, and of chains and imprisonment. They were stoned, they were sawn in two, were tempted, were slain with the sword. They wandered about in sheepskins and goatskins, being destitute, afflicted, tormented— of whom the world was not worthy. They wandered in deserts and mountains, in dens and caves of the earth* (Hebrews 11:32-38).

THE GREAT COMMISSION

It is sobering to remember that God had commissioned Israel to be a light to the Gentiles in showing forth His ways. They were to be kept separate unto the Lord and not adopt the pagan practices around them. But as a nation they were disobedient, and so had their lamp stand taken away from them. Not only this, they were given a spirit of stupor with no revelation (Isaiah 6:9-10).

But we are not going to be like Israel. We are going to stand with Jesus as He commissioned us to continue His work:

> *"All authority has been given to Me in heaven and on earth. Go therefore and make disciples of all the nations, baptizing them in the name of the Father and of the Son and of the Holy Spirit, teaching them to observe all things that I have commanded you; and lo, I am with you always, even to the end of the age"* (Matthew 28:18-20).

As the age comes to a close, what part has the Lord asked you to play, for surely you are to be the light and salt to the people around you? These are perilous time, Paul warned Timothy, for men will be lovers of themselves and adopt many selfish traits. This is the age of narcissism and selfies – don't get caught up in it and other distractions. We need the Holy Spirit to keep us from the world's seductions and anything that would hinder us from fulfilling our mission.

The in-filling of the Holy Spirit and the gifts of the Holy Spirit are alive and in real operation today. For a believer, if you don't believe you can't receive. If you don't believe the gifts are real and God is still using people supernaturally, then you don't have to be concerned with being used in that manner. It is always by faith that we receive from God … we receive our salvation by faith and the gifts by faith.

I remember telling my congregation that God loves you so much, He will not allow you to go to hell. Why would you want to spend eternity with a God you don't know and you don't love? Think about it … it is God's desire that none should perish; nevertheless some people will reject God and spend eternity in hell. In the same way, if you don't believe in the gifts of the Spirit, you don't have to worry about operating in these gifts.

We need the Holy Spirit both to dwell in us and to empower us to rise above our natural weakness. Above all, we need to embrace the love of God so that we will have His compassion to reach a lost and dying world. Many churches preach that the tremendous signs, wonders and miracles that took place in the book of Acts are a thing of the past and we do not need the baptism of the Holy Spirit. Friends, that's a lie from the pit of hell to keep you weak and complacent, and to rob you of your inheritance. We need the Holy Spirit more than ever before to lead us away from evil.

Like Gideon, will you rise up and say with me, "Yes, Holy Spirit, I am ready to receive you in all your power? I am ready to learn more about your gifts and fruit."

Chapter 3

THE FRUIT OF THE SPIRIT
-LOVE, JOY, PEACE-

We saw in the last chapter that to be filled with something means to be under its control. We are greatly influenced by whatever fills us. When we are filled with the Holy Spirit, there is no limit to the new life in Jesus we can experience. However, if we are filled with anger, fear, sorrow, pride, anxiety, these emotions will dominate all our relationships and sour them. Even though we profess our faith, parts of us will still be controlled by the powers of darkness.

RECOGNIZABLE BY THEIR FRUIT

Jesus made it clear that true followers of Christ will be **recognizable by their fruit.** Our fruit can be either good or bad depending on the tree. Didn't Jesus warn us?

> *"A good tree cannot bear bad fruit, nor can a bad tree bear good fruit. Do men gather grapes from thornbushes or figs from thistles? Even so, every good tree bears good fruit, but a bad tree bears bad fruit. A good tree cannot bear bad fruit, nor can a bad tree bear good fruit. Every tree that does not bear good fruit is cut down and thrown into the fire. Therefore by their fruits you will know them"* (Matthew 7:16-20).

Fruit is the direct result of whatever controls our hearts ... for whatever comes out of our mouth will water the seed we planted. Listen again to Jesus:

> *"Do you not yet understand that whatever enters the mouth goes into the stomach and is eliminated? But those things which proceed out of the mouth come from the heart, and they defile a man. For out of the heart proceed evil thoughts, murders, adulteries, fornications, thefts, false witness, blasphemies"* (Matthew 15:17-19).

When we have committed ourselves to Jesus Christ and live to please Him, we will make behavioral choices that look like His. A fruitful Christian will produce life-giving fruit. But if we choose to remain in the flesh, our sinful passions will yield death-producing fruit.

> *For when we were in the flesh, the sinful passions which were aroused by the law were at work in our members to bear fruit to death* (Romans 7:5).

What kind of fruit produces life or death? Galatians 5 gives two lists startling in their contrast.

WORKS OF THE FLESH

The first list describes the **works of the flesh.** These are the acts that may have characterized our lives before we came to Christ. The fruit of a life not surrendered to Jesus include the following:

> *Now the works of the flesh are evident, which are: adultery, fornication, uncleanness, lewdness, idolatry, sorcery, hatred, contentions, jealousies, outbursts of wrath, selfish ambitions, dissensions, heresies, envy, murders, drunkenness, revelries, and the like; of*

which I tell you beforehand, just as I also told you in time past, **that those who practice such things will not inherit the kingdom of God** (Galatians 5:19-21, emphasis added).

We are to confess, repent of, and, with God's help, overcome such acts. Let's look at them more closely:

Sexual immorality: whoredom, fornication, and idolatry. It means a surrendering of sexual purity, and it is primarily used of premarital sexual relations.

Impurity: uncleanness ... the decaying influence of moral (spiritual) impurity; becoming "corrupt"

Debauchery: excessive indulgence in sensual pleasures, crazy partying and wild nights, usually accompanied by a lot of alcohol

Idolatry: worship of idols – car, money, job, kids

Witchcraft: manipulation or control of another

Hatred: intense dislike or ill will towards another

Discord: contentious disagreement between people

Jealousy: the state or feeling of wanting what someone has

Fits of rage: violent and uncontrolled anger

I remember hearing a story about a football player who was so upset about a mistake on the football field, he went into the locker room and in a fit of rage ... he tore up the locker room!

When you use your energy in the game, that's great! What makes this case stand out is everybody is watching you on the field. He told the reporter he couldn't help himself. But he could control himself enough to do it when no one was watching.

Selfish ambition: motivation to elevate oneself or to put one's own interests before another's. We are told: *"Let nothing be done*

through selfish ambition or conceit, but in lowliness of mind let each esteem others better than himself" (Philippians 2:3).

Dissensions: disagreement that leads to discord... It's okay to "agree to disagree."

Envy: desire to have a quality, possession, or other desirable attribute belonging to someone else

Drunkenness: the state of being intoxicated and losing control over one's behavior

Orgies: wild parties, especially one involving excessive drinking and unrestrained sexual activity **... and the like:** pornography and masturbation... BEAT IT, Bro! You can't be like MJ! BEAT IT, Sis... BUZZZ THINGS that take batteries!

Don't see your particular works of the flesh in the above list? Well, they are covered in the phrase ... **and the like!**

FRUIT OF THE SPIRIT

Contrasted with the acts of the flesh, are the fruit of the Spirit of God. These are not individual "fruits" which we pick and choose at will. Rather, the fruit of the Spirit comes in a cluster of nine "fruit" that characterize all who truly walk in the Holy Spirit.

> *But the fruit of the Spirit is love, joy, peace, longsuffering, kindness, goodness, faithfulness, gentleness, self-control. Against such there is no law* (Galatians 5:22–23).

When I think about fruit, two things come to mind. One is that a tree brings forth its fruit naturally, not by compulsion – that would be legalism. We can now produce good fruit naturally because our tree, the Tree of Life, is good. Our good fruit are in stark contrast to the acts of the flesh we used to indulge in. Some of these acts, like gossip and hitting back, seemed so natural at one time only because they were in the nature of that kind of tree. For then we were growing on the Tree of the Knowledge of Good and Evil, a tree planted by Lucifer, which could only produce bad fruit.

Secondly, we will continuously bring forth our fruit in season as we allow the Holy Spirit to work in us. We will also see a gradual improvement in size, taste, color and texture because we are being transformed into His likeness.

Now that we have experienced salvation in Jesus Christ, these are the products that should characterize our lives. But for a while there will be a battle going on between our spirit (which is saved) and our soulish nature which still wants to hold on to Galatians 5:19-21. The devil doesn't want you to know that you CAN have victory over his wiles and temptations with God's strength! He doesn't want you to understand that you've been given a free will – the choice to either believe his lies or allow God's truth to set you free. Choose to walk in the Spirit:

> *I say then: "Walk in the Spirit, and you shall not fulfill the lust of the flesh.* **For the flesh lusts against the Spirit, and the Spirit against the flesh; and these are contrary to one another, so that you do not do the things that you wish.** *But if you are led by the Spirit, you are not under the law* (Galatians 5:16-18, emphasis added).

When you finally surrender to being led by the Spirit, what a liberating experience! That bar or night club you used to frequent with your buddies not longer has the same pull. Those porn sites you would secretly visit – you now feel a check in your spirit. That reading group you attended, which was really a gossip center, simply repels you. You do this not out of any compulsion but because your tastes are changing. You see, while the law compels you to do things against your inner desires, the law of Christ as in Galatians 6:2 gives you the freedom to break out of sin.

Keep up the fight. Your sinful flesh will still wrestle with you as the Holy Spirit draws you to produce His kind of fruit. Paul, writing to the church at Ephesus, urges us to put off our former conduct, which he calls "**the old man**" which grows corrupt according to deceitful lusts. Instead, we are to be renewed in our mind, and put on "**the new man**" which is the nature God intended for us, in true righteousness and holiness (see Ephesians 4:22-24).

The fruit of the Spirit is therefore a rich display of grace, conduct and character springing from our roots in Christ. In order to mature as believers, it's important that we study and understand the attributes of each of the nine fruit. In this chapter we will examine the first three: Love, Joy and Peace.

LOVE

The first fruit is love. Love is of paramount importance because it is the sap produced by the tree of life that nourishes all the other fruit. Without the outflow of love in all our relationships, the other fruit would be an empty show.

The English word "love" has a very broad meaning, but in *the* Greek language there are different kinds of love. The love which the Holy Spirit nurtures in believers is called *agape,* which is often translated as "unconditional love." This love is not a feeling but a choice, the choice of being kind, selfless, considerate, enduring.

> *Love endures with patience and serenity, love is kind and thoughtful, and is not jealous or envious; love does not brag and is not proud or arrogant. It is not rude; it is not self-seeking, it is not provoked [nor overly sensitive and easily angered]; it does not take into account a wrong endured. It does not rejoice at injustice, but rejoices with the truth [when right and truth prevail]. Love bears all things [regardless of what comes], believes all things [looking for the best*

in each one], hopes all things [remaining steadfast during difficult times], endures all things [without weakening]. Love never fails [it never fades nor ends] (1 Corinthians 13:4-8 AMP).

Do you remember Jesus talking about love and saying that it was easy to love those who are good to you? But to love those who treat you harshly even to the point of persecuting you? Ah, that's another matter! If we were to rely on our survival instincts, when someone strikes us, we would retaliate by striking back. But now that we are "Christian" we know that is wrong, so we do nothing and suffer in silence. Already that hints of legalism. But didn't Jesus go beyond human nature and take love to another level? (He's still working on me)

But I say to you, love your enemies, bless those who curse you, do good to those who hate you, and pray for those who spitefully use you and persecute you, that you may be sons of your Father in heaven; for He makes His sun rise on the evil and on the good, and sends rain on the just and on the unjust. For if you love those who love you, what reward have you? Do not even the tax collectors do the same? And if you greet your brethren only, what do you do more than others? Do not even the tax collectors do so? Therefore you shall be perfect, just as your Father in heaven is perfect (Matthew 5:44-48).

Wow! That's tough! Even if I strain myself to be nice to such a person outwardly, inwardly I would still have great reservations about "loving" them. My friend, Jesus is not asking you to be lovey-dovey towards nasty people; that would be hypocritical. He wants you to ask for God's love for them so that you can see beyond their bad behavior to their hurts and need for healing. Then you can treat them with compassion and pray for them. You see, we are not asked to be right. But we are asked to be **perfect** – like our Father. And, if Jesus said it can be done, then we are going to ask the Holy Spirit to take over and translate our limited human love into God's perfect supernatural love. With God all things are possible! There is hope for me and you!

You will see *agape* in operation in all of the "hard" love verses in the New Testament:

> *"Greater love has no one than this, that one lay down his life for his friends"* (John 15:13).
>
> *"Love your enemies, do good to them, and lend to them without expecting to get anything back"* (Luke 6:35).
>
> *And so we know and rely on the love God has for us. God is love. Whoever lives in love lives in God, and God in him* (1 John 4:16).

It is because of love that God carried out His plan to save the world:

> *For God so loved the world that He gave His only begotten Son, that whoever believes in Him shall not perish, but have eternal life* (John 3:16).

It is only by God's love that we can keep the greatest commandments: "*Love the Lord your God*" and "*... love your neighbor as yourself*" (Mark 12:30-31). Through Jesus Christ, our greatest goal is to do all things in love.

Sincere and Authentic Love

At New Beginning Ministries my husband and I taught on LOVE for an entire year. The theme for that year was "Let Love Win." We went out of our way as a congregation to be intentional about showing love to others even when it was tough.

That reminds me of a quote from Maya Angelou: "I've learned that people will forget what you said, people will forget what you did, but people will never forget how you made them feel." Please be genuine and authentic … people can feel if you are sincere with your manner and actions and not see you as a phony saint.

Father, we so much want to please You by loving others the way You love us. We know this is impossible in the natural no matter how much we try. But we have the Holy Spirit and we ask for a heart of compassion that only You can give. We receive it now by faith, in Jesus' name! AMEN!!

JOY

The second characteristic listed is joy. "Joy" in Greek is *chara*, which is a feeling of inner gladness, delight or rejoicing. Joy is the natural response to the work of God and expresses a deep sense of fulfillment in God's kingdom of *"righteousness, peace and joy in the Holy Spirit"* (Romans 14:17).

The Holy Spirit produces joy in several ways:

- **The joy of salvation**

    Being born again is a joyful experience. Most new believers would agree that, upon giving their lives to Jesus, they felt a certain lightness and great joy. God has filled a void in our life or lifted burdens off us that were too heavy. When I can think of nothing to rejoice about, I think of my salvation – that God should save a wretch like me!

    In the Book of Acts, the multitudes thronged to Philip the evangelist in the city of Samaria when word got around about the miracles he did. Many were delivered of unclean spirits and many who were paralyzed and lame were healed. *"And there was great joy in that city"* because of the saving power of God (see Acts 8:5-8).

    All heaven, too, rejoices when a sinner returns to the Lord. Imagine the Father seeing the prodigal son from afar, running out to meet him and embracing him – pigsty smell and all! All the young man ever expected was to be treated as a servant but the Father restored to him the full honor of sonship (see Luke 15:11-31).

- **The joy of growing in a relationship**

Jesus said, *"These things I have spoken to you, that My joy may **remain** in you, and that your joy may be full"* (John 15:11, emphasis added).

How do we hold on to the joy of our first encounter with Jesus? Through abiding in Him. That is mainly through the word. Knowing about Him is not enough: we need to know Him intimately. The Holy Spirit will bring light to us as we study the word. He will give us special insight into our circumstances and He will cause a flow of communication with Him as He lights up that word. This is the start of a growing intimacy with the Lord.

He leads us through paths of righteousness as we know Him and obey His commandments. He takes us to that secret place of the Most High God, where we receive protection and safety. He comforts us in our pain through His fellowship. He takes us to the heights of worship as enter into His presence with praise, and He stills our hearts as we meditate on His promises. In His presence there is fullness of joy as expressed by David the psalmist: *In Your presence is fullness of joy; At Your right hand are pleasures forevermore* (Psalm 16:11).

As we know Him more intimately, we are transformed according to His image (See 2 Corinthians 3:18). And, collectively, as believers, when we unite in demonstrating the mind, love, and purpose of Christ, we bring joy to others. We see this in Paul encouraging the church to complete his joy by having the same motivation, the same love, the same mind: *"… fulfill my joy by being like-minded, having the same love, being of one accord, of one mind"* (Philippians 2:2).

- *The joy of deliverance*

   When God sets someone free, this is indeed cause for celebration.

   Hannah had been barren for many years and cried out in anguish to the Lord. She vowed that if He gave her conception she would dedicate her son to His service. Samuel was born. And now, she was bringing her three-year old toddler to the temple to fulfill that vow. It must have been heart-wrenching to be separated from her first born, but she was joyful to be delivered of barrenness and blessed with fruitfulness: *"My heart rejoices in the LORD; my horn is exalted in the LORD"* (1 Samuel 2:1).

   At Philippi, Paul and Silas were severely beaten and then put into prison for disturbing the peace. In their stocks in the inner prison, you would expect them to be sitting in grim silence nursing their wounds, expecting the worst. But this is not what they did. They were praising and singing hymns so loud the whole prison could hear! With their grateful hearts, they were already stepping into the realm of the miraculous. Suddenly there was an earthquake and immediately all the prison doors were opened and the prisoners' chains were loosed. As a result the jailor gave his life to Jesus together with his entire household (Acts 16:25-31).

- **The joy in adversity**

   Surprisingly, the apostle James tells us to *"count it all joy"* when we fall into various trials. What an amazing statement – to be joyful in adversity! "Yes," James would say, "That's so important, I made it the opening statement of my book. I'll say it again ..."

   > *My brethren, count it all joy when you fall into various trials, knowing that the testing of your*

> *faith produces patience. But let patience have its perfect work, that you may be perfect and complete, lacking nothing* (James 1:2-8).

Look closely at this opening statement. Do you see three of the fruit of the Holy Spirit already at work? Yes, you recognized them: joy, faith and patience. What James is saying is that adversity tests our faith, and the fitting response should be joy. Why? Because the testing of our faith produces patience. And when patience is developed, the **final product** is perfection.

The Greek word for "perfect" is *teleios*, which means "having reached the end" or "term," and therefore "complete," "full," "perfect." When we all come to the unity of the faith and of the knowledge of the Son of God, we arrive at the perfect man, reflecting the stature of the fullness of Christ (see Ephesians 4:13). This is not likely to happen in our lifetime but we must continually strive towards that goal.

I find the idea of rejoicing in tribulation truly an extraordinary concept which cannot be explained by human reasoning. But the Bible tells us to be joyful in adversity. This is not because of the pain but the assurance that it is going to produce the kind of patience that will develop the character the Holy Spirit wants to build in us. We ought to continually set our eyes toward perfection, looking to Him who is able to make us complete in every good work to do His will, working in us what is well pleasing in His sight (see Hebrews 13:21).

No wonder Jesus looked to the cross with joy, seeing in the distant future the souls that would be won over to the kingdom! Similarly, let us run our race with joy seeing at the end the completion of Christ's work in us.

> *... let us run with endurance the race that is set before us, looking unto Jesus, the author and finisher of our faith, who for the joy that was set*

before Him endured the cross, despising the shame, and has sat down at the right hand of the throne of God (Hebrews 12:1-2).

PEACE

The New Testament word for "peace" in Greek is usually *eirene*. *Eirene* is similar in many ways to the Hebrew *shalom*. It means, not just freedom from unrest, but freedom to be everything that promotes a man's highest good, spiritually, materially, mentally, emotionally. The Old Testament anticipated, and the New Testament confirmed, that God's peace would be mediated through a Messiah, that is, through the death and resurrection of Jesus Christ. Peter declared to Cornelius at the time he received Jesus that peace came through Jesus Christ, the Lord of all (see **Acts 10:36**-37).

However, peace is not something inherent in our human nature, for we were born at war. At birth, our sinful nature has already declared war on God and His truth. Our heart's desire was to be separated from Him and, if we persisted in this desire until death, we would get what we wanted – separation from Him for all eternity.

But God's methods of warfare are not what we expect. Instead of a battle, He sent us the Prince of Peace:

> *For unto us a Child is born,*
> *Unto us a Son is given;*
> *And the government will be upon His shoulder.*
> *And His name will be called*
> *Wonderful, Counselor, Mighty God,*
> *Everlasting Father, Prince of Peace* (Isaiah 9:6).

Jesus' goal in coming to earth was more than simply to cease hostilities. He came to bring about a full and abiding relationship of restoration and love. The cost of this peace was His life.

> *But He was wounded for our transgressions, He was bruised for our iniquities; the chastisement for our peace was upon Him, And by His stripes we are healed* (Isaiah 53:5).

Romans 3:10b-11 explains man's rejection of Christ: *"None is righteous, no, not one; no one understands; no one seeks for God. All have turned aside; together they have become worthless ..."* (ESV).

The truth is none of us can accept Jesus' offer of peace based on our own will and power. Our natural selves reject it. Only God can initiate a desire for peace with Him. It's the Holy Spirit who leads us to want Jesus and His message. Once the Spirit draws us, we believe in Jesus, and the peace follows: *"Therefore, having been justified by faith, we have peace with God through our Lord Jesus Christ"* (Romans 5:1).

And not only do we have peace with God, we have the ability to have peace with our fellow men. Paul exhorts us to the best of our ability to live peaceably with all (see Romans 12:18). What a perfect example of our role in showing Christ to the world!

The fruit of the Spirit includes a peace that goes beyond that of being saved. It is a sweet relationship because we are now God's friends (see John 15:15). We have access to His presence (see Ephesians 2:11-18) and can confidently approach Him directly to seek His mercy and grace in time of need (see Hebrews 4:16). As we fix our thoughts on Him, He will keep us in perfect peace: *"You will keep him in perfect peace, whose mind is stayed on You, because he trusts in You"* (Isaiah 26:3).

Since God's peace transcends earthly matters, we do not have to worry but bring our petition before the Lord. Having done that, we are to let the peace of God take control of our mind.

> *Be anxious for nothing, but in everything by prayer and supplication, with thanksgiving, let your requests*

be made known to God; and the peace of God, which surpasses all understanding, will guard your hearts and minds through Christ Jesus (Philippians 4:6-7).

It's a peace that the world cannot give – to the worldly mind, such peace is incomprehensible. It transcends all understanding. It's the peace that Christ has left with us.

"Peace I leave with you, My peace I give to you; not as the world gives do I give to you. Let not your heart be troubled, neither let it be afraid" (John 14:27).

I pray that God fill you with all joy and peace as you trust in Him, so that you may overflow with hope by the power of the Holy Spirit! (see Romans 15:13)

My Peace in the Midst of Storms

I am a witness to the peace that passes all understanding. In 1996 the enemy came at me with all he could throw at me. I had a JOB EXPERIENCE for real.

In March my mother-in-law passed away. We had a good relationship but the strain it put on my husband affected our family, resulting in the marriage breaking down. I was devastated by the divorce since we had been friends since I was fifteen years old. Then in August the building in which my business was housed was sold, so my business had to close down and my business partner and I had to rent space in another salon. The transition was costly in terms of start-up and building a whole new clientele.

The biggest tragedy was about to come. On Christmas Eve that year my daughter passed away. She was my only child and passed away from complications from away from complications from Sickle Cell Disease (SCD) Yes, I mourned the loss of my daughter Meesha Chanell Saxton … BUT the peace of God came over me and I did not lose my mind. You see, I had been infertile and we finally had Meesha after many years of trying to get pregnant.

NOW THAT KNOCKED THE WIND out of me ... I became DEPRESSED!!! The sad part was I did not even know that I was depressed. I just knew I did not feel like myself. BUT the peace of God kept me ... No, I could not attend baby showers or kids' parties (that was just too painful) – even to see kids around the age of two was hard for me. BUT the peace of God kept me.

All I can say is when the scripture says His yoke is easy and His burdens are light, the peace of God that passes all understanding keeps us.

Satan came at me hard again. In February 1997 my mother suffered two brain aneurisms. I had had enough. That's when I rose up in my spirit and took authority. I remember being in the ICU waiting room and the doctors coming to my Dad and me, telling us there was nothing more they could do for my mother. A HOLY BOLDNESS stood up in me and I stood up right there in the ICU waiting room and starting telling God what His word said. I decreed and declared that my mother WOULD LIVE AND NOT DIE. I DECREED AND DECLARED that the Lord would not put more on me that I could bear and that I could not bear losing my mother. "NOT NOW, LORD!" I decreed and declared that satan and the spirit of death take their hands off my mother right now, in the name of Jesus!

About an hour later the doctors came and said my mother's condition was turning around ... that she was a fighter. GLORY!!! My mother Gertrude Huey lived 7 more years after that day.

CONCLUSION

In closing, let us remember that the Holy Spirit makes a heavy demand on us when He opens His cluster of fruit, starting with the fruit of love. Not any kind of love but God's *agape* love – a costly love that does not count the cost. If we want the rest of the fruit, we will first have to pass the test of trading our human love for this radical love. Once we have made that decision and asked for it, we can expect the Holy Spirit to start a supernatural work in us, one that defies reason. The release of this power to love the unlovable will show the world that God is at work. This person is being transformed and moving to a different drumbeat. Will it happen? Love never fails!

With your heart already open to love, you are filled with a joy that smiles at affliction and a peace that surpasses understanding. Are you ready to receive more fruit?

Chapter 4

THE FRUIT OF THE HOLY SPIRIT
-PATIENCE, KINDNESS, GOODNESS-

The works of the flesh and the fruit of the Holy Spirit – oh, what a stark contrast! It's as if a wild animal was fighting with a tame one within the same person. And so they were. The kingdom of darkness in our unregenerate soul was raging against our new nature in Christ.

In this chapter we are going to look at three more fruit of the Holy Spirit. But before that, I would like to single out among the works of the flesh, one group that is built around anger. I am doing this to give a dramatic illustration of the power of evil operating within just one emotion, and the many tentacles it puts out.

Let's have another look at the works of the flesh in the Amplified version.

> *Now the practices of the sinful nature are clearly evident: they are sexual immorality, impurity, sensuality (total irresponsibility, lack of self-control), idolatry, sorcery, hostility, strife, jealousy,* **fits of anger, disputes, dissensions, factions [that promote heresies]***, envy, drunkenness, riotous behavior, and other things like these* (Galatians 5:16-26 AMP, emphasis added).

So we are looking at the following works under the core emotion, anger: fits of anger, disputes, dissensions, factions.

Blinded by Anger

"Fits of anger" describes violent and uncontrolled rage. The Greek word for it is *thymós* and it indicates the personal venting of anger. Interestingly, *thymós* is also used of God's perfect, holy wrath (see Revelation 14:10, 19; 15:1). Jesus, too, experienced *thymós* on many occasions but it was always under control from manifesting in intense rage. This is holy anger, directed against sin with intense opposition, and is without sin: *"Be angry, **and** do not sin ..."* (Ephesians 4:26).

Have you ever had somebody look you straight in the eye and **LIE**? The look was so sincere ... you were taken in. You felt betrayed ... then you realized they were not lying to you but to themselves! The same goes for anger. When you give vent to explosive anger all the time, you are not just hurting others, you are doing violence to yourself. If uncontrollable anger is an issue with you, God wants to totally heal you today. It starts with admitting you have an issue. It is hard to admit it when it's your normal behavior which you see as an integral part of your personality.

I did my Applied Business Degree internship at a domestic violence women's shelter called the Green House in Chardon. Here, I worked in the community to help bring awareness about the many victims of rage in its various forms. Here are some of the more common ones in overt and subtle forms. Maybe you were victim to some of them, or maybe you were the perpetrator.

> **Physical Abuse:** a punch or a kick, stabbing, shooting, choking, slapping, forcing you to use drugs
>
> **Emotional Abuse:** an attempt to destroy the victim's self-worth, and is brought about by persistent insult, humiliation, or criticism
>
> The saying "Sticks and stones may break my bones but words will never hurt me" is a downright LIE. Look at what the bible says: *"There is one whose rash words are like sword thrusts ..."* (Proverbs 12:18).

Sexual Abuse: not just sexual assault and rape, but also harassment, such as unwelcome touching and other demeaning behaviors.

Financial Abuse: simply another form of control, preventing the victim from seeking financial freedom, for example, in obtaining an education or a job outside the home.

Psychological Abuse: basically a catchall term for intimidating, threatening, or fear-causing behavior.

If anger is not checked at the personal level, it can escalate to displays of anger at the social level and stir up an angry crowd, or provoke dissension and sedition. Uncontrolled anger can lead to:

Disputes: hostile disagreements, arguments, or debates; a continual readiness and proneness to quarrelling. Disputes, if not checked can lead to fights or physical violence to persons or property.

Dissensions: disagreements that lead to discord or unrest; dividing into parties, which in the state lead to factions, and in the church to church splits

Factions: conflicting groups within an organization; small, organized, dissenting groups within a larger entity, especially in politics or within the church that promote heresies

Heresies: beliefs or opinions contrary to orthodox views and are without any foundation in the word of God. They spring from a corrupt and carnal mind, and are fed by popular approval.

The following episode from the book of Acts illustrates how disagreement with Paul's teaching among certain individuals quickly escalated into violence.

Paul was preaching in the synagogue in Thessalonica. Reasoning with them from the Scriptures, he declared that Jesus is the Messiah, and many Jews and Gentiles were persuaded to follow him. However, other Jews were jealous, so they rounded up some bad characters from the marketplace, formed a mob and started a riot in the city.

These Jews could not accept the views put forward by Paul but they were too angry to reason with him in a civilized way. Why were they angry? Most likely, they couldn't stand the thought of the Gentiles inheriting the kingdom – if they the chosen ones couldn't have it, why should anyone else have it (that's envy, another work of the flesh)? So they whipped up a mob, accusing Paul and his team of defying Caesar's decrees by claiming that Jesus was King (see Acts 17:1-8).

What does the word of God say about this volatile emotion?

Do not be eager in your heart to be angry,

For anger dwells in the heart of fools (Ecclesiastes 7:9, AMP).

… for anger resteth in the bosom of fools (KJV).

If you can't control your anger, the bible says you are a fool. When anger wants to crawl up and go to bed, it has to find a FOOL'S heart … I wonder who they are talking about?

The hardest thing to get out of is a HEART THING. Why? Because it always has reasons; it justifies itself: "I have a reason to be like this."

"You see, my father was like this – he beat me." "She cheated on me"… "They hurt me"… "She lied on me" …"He broke my heart" …"I was molested"… "I don't know my father!"

So you say you can't help it – you've been conditioned to behave in that way because your dad or mom did. My friend, if you have been saved, then you can help it. The truth is, anger kills its landlord. You are at the mercy of the ins and outs of life, the ups and downs, the *ying* and *yang*. One minute you're praising God in church … falling out in the spirit … but get in the parking lot and you're going off at someone who blocked your car! If you don't kill anger, it will kill you!

Anger often carries a license … and you can't confiscate the weapon because it has a license. You see, as long as we continue to justify ourselves, we will never be set free. But he who rules his own spirit is mightier than he who rules a city:

He who is slow to anger is better than the mighty, And he who rules his spirit than he who takes a city (Proverbs 16:32).

So, tell me, how do I manage emotions? How do I go through the feelings and not react in a certain way. Is it possible?

One thing you should not do is suppress your emotions. Emotions are essentially good because they are a barometer of the state of our souls. They make us aware of our inclinations and vulnerabilities. And women are not the only one with emotions. In a recent poll among men who were asked whether they wanted intimacy or sex, the majority said intimacy. Men, too, need to feel loved and accepted.

So emotions are natural human responses to situations; they may even arise from good motives. Your anger may be justified. But deal with it in the appropriate way. Do not allow it to overwhelm you. If you do, you are giving place to the devil, in other words, you are giving him a foothold in your life.

Learn to manage what is managing you ... before it destroys you. We can explode or shut down, we can retaliate by withholding sex or money from our loved ones. Or we can confront it at the root asking, "Why am I really angry?" If anger stays in you, it is the root cause of many illnesses, depression, eating disorders, anxiety, bitterness, discontentment, frustration.

How do you kill anger? The human way is to retaliate. God's way is surprising: act in the opposite direction:

> *Bless those who persecute you; bless and do not curse... Repay no one evil for evil... Beloved, do not avenge yourselves, but rather* **give place to wrath**; *for it is written, "Vengeance is Mine, I will repay," says the Lord. Therefore*
>
>> *"If your enemy is hungry, feed him;*
>> *If he is thirsty, give him a drink;*
>> *For in so doing you will heap coals of fire on his head."*

Do not be overcome by evil, but overcome evil with good (Romans 12:14, 17,19-21).

Do not add fuel to the fire; rather, diffuse the situation. Remember that vengeance belongs to the Lord and He will fight your battles for you. If you want to be a vigilante and fight this battle on your own, then you are fighting in the flesh using your carnal weapons:

> *For the weapons of our warfare are not carnal but mighty in God for pulling down strongholds, casting down arguments and every high thing that exalts itself against the knowledge of God, bringing every thought into captivity to the obedience of Christ ... (2 Corinthians 10:4-5).*

Remember, it is in the spirit that you wage your war. When you allow the Holy Spirit to lead you in prayer, you are nullifying all the arguments of the enemy. You are demolishing his plans to subvert and destroy relationships. You are pulling down strongholds of anger and pride. You are submitting every thought and emotion to the invincible word of God.

Now, I ask you, wouldn't you much rather cast this burden on to the Lord because He is so much better at fighting your enemy, the devil? You, on your part, forgive the one who hurt you and release blessing upon them. Let God be God in this situation.

Are you tired of being an angry person Are you sick of the devil walking all over you? Do you want to come out of being a victim of your emotions?

Then say with me:

DEVIL I WANT MY STUFF BACK! I WANT IT ALL BACK!

I feel a breakthrough coming – demons are trembling right now… "We thought we had a fool … we going to have to move … they're getting a breakthrough!"

So how do we kill anger? By moving in the opposite direction. You can only achieve that by allowing the Holy Spirit to grow more of His fruit in you.

FRUIT OF THE HOLY SPIRIT

We are now going to look at three more fruit: patience, kindness and goodness. Here they are in context:

> *love, joy, peace,* **patience, kindness, goodness**, *faithfulness, gentleness, and self-control* (Galatians 5:22).

While the first three, love, joy, peace, spring out of a personal relationship with God, the remaining six tend to show how the depth of that relationship will be tested by indifference, even hate, by those who oppose the gospel. The true believer will not just hold back from retaliation; they will meet the onslaught of evil with good. (Did I mention God is still working on me ☺?)

PATIENCE

"Patience" in Galatians 5:22 literally means "long temper," in the sense of having the ability to control one's emotions for an indefinite period. The KJV translates it as "longsuffering."

A patient person is able to endure much pain and suffering without complaining. A patient person is slow to anger as he waits for God to provide comfort and punish wrongdoing. Since it is a fruit of the Spirit, we can only possess PATIENCE through the power and work of the Holy Spirit in our lives.

Patience comes from a position of power, not weakness. A person may have the ability to take revenge or cause trouble, but patience brings about self-restraint and careful thinking.

On the other hand, losing patience is a sign of weakness. When we break out and demonstrate anger in overt or subtle ways, it shows that we've lost it; we are out of control. But a patient person is always hopeful, expecting some good to come out of every challenge. We are patient through trying situations out of the hope for a coming deliverance. We are patient with a trying person out of compassion. We choose to love that person and want what's best for him.

And, as the Spirit produces patience in us, He is making us more Christ-like. He will deliver us from the evil one and direct us towards the "*steadfastness and patience of Christ.*"

> *Finally, brothers and sisters ... [pray] that we will be rescued from perverse and evil men; for not everyone has the faith. But the Lord is faithful, and He will strengthen you [setting you on a firm foundation] and will protect and guard you from the evil one ... May the Lord direct your hearts into the love of God and into the steadfastness and patience of Christ* (2 Thessalonians 3:2-5 AMP).

Jesus told His disciples "*By your patience possess your soul.*" This was not a logical explanation but it came at the brink of Jesus going to the cross and alerting them to the fearful signs of the end times. It comes with the warning of great persecution that will come upon all genuine followers of Jesus.

> *"You will be betrayed even by parents and brothers, relatives and friends; and they will put some of you to death ... And you will be hated by all for My name's sake"* (Luke 21:6, 17).

Then come His comforting words

> *"But not a hair of your head shall be lost.* **By your patience possess your souls**.
>
> *Then they will see the Son of Man coming in a cloud with power and great glory. Now when these things begin to happen, look up and lift up your heads, because* **your redemption** *draws nea*r" (Luke 21:18, 9, 27-28).

In these end times, we are already seeing the nations being shaken one after another. We see lawlessness rising up in an unprecedented way; we see perversions and persecution. We see the increasing momentum of the anti-Christ system taking center stage. But we who believe in the words of Jesus will be patient and steadfast. We will not be troubled but wait in faith for His coming in all His glory. Then we will lift up our heads because our final redemption has come.

Even now, Christ is patiently awaiting the completion of the Father's plan. For, after Jesus *"had offered for all time one sacrifice for sins, he sat down at the right hand of God, and since that time he waits for his enemies to be made his footstool"* (Hebrews 10:12-13 NIV). Let us receive His patience.

KINDNESS

The fifth characteristic, kindness, is called "gentleness" in the KJV. The Hebrew word for it is *hesed* which can be interpreted as "lovingkindness," "steadfast love," and "covenant faithfulness." The Greek word for "kindness" is *chrēstotēs,* which means "benignity," "tender concern," "uprightness." Kindness is closely linked with patience: *"love suffers **long** and is **kind**"* (1 Corinthians 13:4). It covers both kindness of heart and kindness of act and this includes the "law of kindness" as can be seen in the conversation of the virtuous woman (see Proverbs 31:26).

Kindness is so close to God's heart because it is the very quality that leads Him to provide salvation for us. It is God's kindness that leads us to repentance (see Romans 2:4, ESV)

> *But when the kindness and the love of God our Savior toward man appeared, not by works of righteousness which we have done, but according to His mercy He saved us ...* (Titus 3:4-5).

Through His kindness, the Lord our Shepherd leads us to green pastures beside the quiet waters, where He restores our weary souls as Psalm 23:2-3 describes. It is God's tender care that makes Him want to gather us under His wings, to protect us and keep us close to Him (see Psalm 91).

David's Kindness to Mephibosheth

There are many examples of kindness in the Bible. One of the most touching is the story of Mephibosheth in the second book of Samuel.

Mephibosheth was the son of King Saul's son Jonathan, David's home boy from back in the day. Jonathan was killed in battle when Mephibosheth was only five years old. Fearing that the Philistines would come for the young boy, his nurse fled with him to safety, but in her haste she dropped him and both of his feet became crippled.

When David became king he asked whether there was still someone of the house of Saul, to whom he might show the kindness of God. So they brought Mephibosheth to him. On seeing him, Mephibosheth prostrated himself before the king and said, *"What is your servant, that you should look upon such a dead dog as I?"*

But David received him kindly and promised to look after him and his household all the days of his life. In spite of all the tragedy surrounding Mephibosheth, his story ends happily:

> *"As for Mephibosheth," said the king, "he shall eat at my table like one of the king's sons." Mephibosheth had a young son whose name was Micha ... So Mephibosheth dwelt in Jerusalem, for he ate continually at the king's table. And he was lame in both his feet* (see 2 Samuel 9:1-13).

In the gospels we have an outstanding example of kindness to a total stranger.

Jesus, preaching on loving one's neighbor, was asked who his neighbor was. So He told this parable of a traveler, who was waylaid by thieves and left as dead. A priest, followed by a Levite, came down that road and passed by on the other side (see Luke 10:30-32).

But a certain Samaritan saw him, and had compassion.

> *"So he went to him and bandaged his wounds, pouring on oil and wine; and he set him on his own animal, brought*

> *him to an inn, and took care of him. On the next day, when he departed, he took out two denarii, gave them to the innkeeper, and said to him, 'Take care of him; and whatever more you spend, when I come again, I will repay you.'*
>
> *So which of these three do you think was neighbor to him who fell among the thieves?*
>
> *And he said, 'He who showed mercy on him.'*
>
> *Then Jesus said to him, 'Go and do likewise'"* (Luke 10:33-37).

How ironic that we have two religious men who chose to ignore the badly injured man, for whatever reason! Perhaps they did not want to soil their garments with blood or defile themselves if this man was already dead. This reminds me at once of Jesus' rebuke of the Pharisees for their hypocrisy in elevating the trivial and external things, while neglecting *"the weightier matters of the law: **justice and mercy and faith**"* (Matthew 23:23, emphasis added).

But here comes a Samaritan, a man from a social group despised by the Jews. He has compassion! He, too, is a busy man but he treats the man's wounds and takes him to an inn to be cared for.

What is Jesus saying?

The mark of the true follower of Jesus is the law of love written in his heart. The Spirit of Christ dwells in him and Christ's compassion renews his soul. He acts with selfless disregard for his own comfort; he makes no distinction as to nationality, ethnic group or status. If we really want to be followers of Jesus in word and deed, then we should demonstrate such compassion, according to our ability, to help, and relieve those who are distressed as they come to us.

GOODNESS

The Greek word for "goodness," *agathosune*, is defined as "uprightness of heart and life." *Agathosune* goes beyond goodness simply for the sake of being virtuous; it is goodness for the benefit of others, an expression of virtue and holiness in action.

Kindness and goodness are also closely linked. The distinction is that, while kindness is an inward disposition i.e. benevolence, goodness is a habitual way of acting i.e. beneficence. It results in a life characterized by deeds motivated by righteousness and a desire to be a blessing.

Expressions of goodness are as varied as the Spirit is creative. Someone with *agathosune* will selflessly act on behalf of others. So is giving to the poor, providing for the education of someone else's children, visiting the sick, volunteering to clear debris after a storm, and praying for the lost. Confronting someone about a sin demonstrates goodness, too. Goodness is also seen in speaking out publicly on behalf of those who have no voice such as children who are the victims of sexual abuse or human trafficking, or defending the right of the unborn child to live, even though it may meet with great opposition.

I told you in Chapter 3 that my daughter Meesha Chanell Saxton passed away from Sickle Cell Disease (SCD) in 1996. Meesha Chanell Saxton was born October 17, 1995 with SCD which is a group of inherited red blood cell disorders. My mother had the sickle cell trait, and I received the sickle gene mutation from her. I did not manifest the disease, neither did my ex-husband but, not knowing he also had the trait, we passed the defective gene on to our daughter Meesha. Due to complications and lack of accurate information about this disease, she passed away on December 24, 1996.

On her behalf I have become an advocate for victims of SCD, a voice for people that do not have one. On my fiftieth birthday I started the Meesha Chanell Saxton Fund (MCS~Fund) in her memory. The sole mission of MCS~FUND is to generate unrestricted funds for Sickle Cell Anemia-affected individuals. Through Supportive Services & Advocacy serving the needs of people plagued by this disease, this is not only a mission, but a passion.

Our vision is to help Sickle Cell Anemia-affected individuals financially as part of Kincaid's Kindred Spirits (KKS) Sickle Cell Anemia Adult Community Outreach. In 2018 we raised over $5000 and by June 19 2019, which is WORLD SICKLE CELL DAY, we plan on raising over $20,000. God is good all the time and all the time God is good! If we have goodness purposed in our heart, God will open supernatural doors for us so that we can be a blessing to others. AMEN!!

CONCLUSION

Patience, kindness and goodness are not qualities we can manufacture on our own. They come from a bountiful God, who gives us every perfect gift (see James 1:17).

And, as others see our good works, they will praise our Father in heaven:

> "*Let your light so shine before men, that they may see your good works and glorify your Father in heaven*" (Matthew 5:16).

People who have patience, kindness and goodness, because they are powered by love, also demonstrate all the qualities of love. They suffer long *and* are kind; they do not envy; do not parade themselves, are not puffed up; do not behave rudely, do not seek their own, are not provoked, think no evil; do not rejoice in iniquity, but rejoice in the truth; they bear all things, believe all things, hope all things, endure all things (see 1 Corinthians 13:4-7).

In closing, let us look someone who was remarkably transformed when the Holy Spirit took over control and gave him back his life. This person was Saul.

Saul started out as a legalistic Pharisee who was driven by his own self-righteousness and hatred for the Way. He was instrumental in persecuting Christians and handing them over to the Sanhedrin. This was the man behind the murder of Stephen. Single-minded in his pursuit, he was on his way to Damascus to arrest more believers when the glory of God struck him. Through the work of the Holy Spirit, his orientation changed from Saul the persecutor of Christians, to Paul apostle of Jesus Christ and servant of the people. His character underwent a dramatic transformation from a man with anger in his heart to a man who could write about and exemplify selfless love as in 1 Corinthians 13.

Towards the end of his life, Paul was ready to lay down his life for the very people he once persecuted:

> *But I will rejoice even if I lose my life, pouring it out like a liquid offering to God, just like your faithful service is an offering to God. And I want all of you to share that joy* (Philippians 2:17 NLT).

Paul had labored tirelessly for their salvation, exposing himself to peril so that both Jews and Gentiles might have the gospel. On their account he had suffered much; he had been made a prisoner at Rome; and there was a possibility, that he might be executed for preaching the gospel. Yet he says that, even if this should happen, he would not regret it, but it would be a source of joy.

Chapter 5

THE FRUIT OF THE SPIRIT
-FAITHFULNESS, GENTLENESS, SELF-CONTROL-

So far we have looked at the first six fruit of the Spirit. Today we are going to look at the final three fruit: faithfulness, gentleness and self-control.

FAITHFULNESS

The word "faith" comes from the Greek word *pistis* and it operates both as a **GIFT** and a **FRUIT**. As a fruit of the Spirit, *pistis* can be translated "faithfulness," the quality of steadfastness, constancy, or allegiance. "Faith" is to trust in what the Bible says about God: His existence, His word and His very character. Therefore "faithfulness" is responding steadfastly to that trust in Him, His word and character.

So how can we cultivate the fruit of faithfulness? By being trustworthy in whatever we have been entrusted to do – from the little to the great. As members of the body of Christ, we all have been assigned different functions to complete the whole. So the fingers can't do what the toes do, neither can the eyes be expected to do what the ears do. The ears can't be telling the eyes, "Why are you looking over there?" Nor can the eyes be telling the ears, "Why are you listening that way; you need to be listening this way." No, you perform your assigned role.

In discussing the fruit of faithfulness, Paul submits that the Christian life is demonstrated in the faithful and honest handling of all things committed to us. We also carry out our function earnestly, with our whole heart, not in a half-hearted way.

Hebrews 11:6 tells us, "... *without faith it is impossible to please Him* ..." It is impossible to say we are faithful to God if we lack faith. In the first place, if we don't have faith, we can't even be in this relationship. We have faith because we believe what the scriptures say about Him and we apply it in our lives. We demonstrate that not only do we believe in His faithfulness, but that we, too, want to be faithful to Him.

I personally have the gift of faith and know that God will give me my heart's desire because He placed those desires in my heart in the first place. I used to think it was the FAVOR of God on my life. That is true but I also operate in the gift of faith. The only way I know how to describe it is that my faith is both strong and in line with God's will upon my life. I find that what I am believing and speaking out of my mouth eventually comes to pass .... it's been that way as long as I can remember.

I had long wanted to go to South Africa on an African safari. So when I took my nephew to Disney World Amusement Park on their African safari, I knew that I would be going to Africa one day on a real safari. Needless to say in 2012, I went on my first trip to South Africa on a mission trip with Marilyn Hickey Ministries and I got my chance to go on an African safari.

On another occasion, while at cosmetology school, I went to hair shows in Atlanta, New York and Chicago. I was so inspired that I could see myself being a platform artist. I also knew in my heart that one day I would be an educator, and then, lo and behold, an educator from L'Oreal professional product division Mizani came into my salon and spa one day selling tickets to a local hair show. She invited me to join their styling team. After many conversations and mulling over it, I knew that I was called to accept this business opportunity. I became a national educator for MIZANI L'Oreal Professional Products live for thirteen years.

I believe my faithfulness to God has been the catalyst for my operating in the gift of faith.

A Relationship Built on Love

What the Bible says about faithfulness has everything to do with the character of God. The Ten Commandments given by God to Moses in Exodus 20 is for all people, for all time.

Notice that the first four commandments are about our relationship with God.

> *And God spoke all these words, saying:*
>
> *I am the Lord your God, who brought you out of the land of Egypt, out of the house of bondage.*
>
> *You shall have no other gods before Me.*
>
> *You shall not make for yourself a carved image—any likeness of anything that is in heaven above, or that is in the earth beneath, or that is in the water under the earth; you shall not bow down to them nor serve them. For I, the Lord your God, am a jealous God, visiting the iniquity of the fathers upon the children to the third and fourth generations of those who hate Me, but showing mercy to thousands, to those who love Me and keep My commandments.*
>
> *You shall not take the name of the LORD your God in vain, for the LORD will not hold him guiltless who takes His name in vain.*
>
> *Remember the Sabbath day, to keep it holy. Six days you shall labor and do all your work, but the seventh*

day is the Sabbath of the LORD your God ... (Exodus 20:2-10).

The above scripture demonstrates a God longing to have a loving relationship with His people. And, just as God is faithful to us, so also does He want us to be faithful to Him.

God's desire for love is embedded in the Ten Commandments. Jesus said that the entire Ten Commandments can be summed in just two: love God and love your neighbor (see Mark 12:30-31). If you love God, you will follow the first four Commandments, and if you love your neighbor, you will want to follow the rest of the Commandments. As we begin to love God, and as we begin to love our neighbor, then we position ourselves to walk in faithfulness.

Benefits of Being Faithful

What are the benefits of walking in faithfulness? Consider these scriptures:

> *For the LORD loves the just and will not forsake his faithful ones* (Psalm 37:28 ASV).
>
> *My son, do not forget my teaching, but keep my commands in your heart, for they will prolong your life many years and bring your prosperity* (Proverbs 3:12 NIV).
>
> *Through love and faithfulness sin is atoned for; through the fear of the LORD a man avoids evil. When a man's ways are pleasing to the LORD, he makes even his enemies live at peace with him* (Proverbs 16:6-7 NIV).

So when we are faithful, we have the assurance that God will

- never forsake us
- give us long life

- give us prosperity
- forgive our sins
- keep us away from evil
- protect us from our enemies

Our faithfulness rests in the unshakeable belief that God is who He says He is, and that we can trust in Him despite the uncertainties of life. Functionally, that means we trust what God says in the Bible, not necessarily what the world or our own eyes tell us. We are going to trust He will work out everything for good (see Romans 8:28). We trust He will work His will in us (Philippians 2:13). And we trust that our situation on earth cannot be compared to our future reward in heaven:

> *Eye has not seen, nor ear heard, nor have entered into the heart of man the things which God has prepared for those who love Him* (1 Corinthians 2:9).

Abiding in Christ

Jesus tells us more about faithfulness in John 15:

> *I am the true **vine**, and My Father is the **vinedresser**. Every **branch** in Me that does not bear fruit He takes away; and every branch that **bears fruit** He prunes, that it may bear more fruit. You are already clean because of the word which I have spoken to you. Abide in Me, and I in you. As the branch cannot bear fruit of itself, unless it abides in the vine, neither can you, unless you abide in Me. I am the vine, you are the branches. He who abides in Me, and I in him, bears much fruit; for without Me you can do nothing. If anyone does not abide in Me, he is cast out as a branch and is withered; and they gather them and throw them into the fire, and they are burned. If you abide in Me, and My words*

abide in you, you will ask what you desire, and it shall be done for you. By this My Father is glorified, that you bear much fruit; so you will be My disciples (John 15:1-8, emphasis added).

It's all about the fruit of the Spirit. Here, I want to cite faithfulness, in particular, because it's that quality of trusting wholly in the Lord that sustains all nine fruit. The only way we can have such a deep trust is through the in-dwelling Spirit of Truth.

In this scripture we see Jesus as the True Vine, ourselves as the branches, and God the Father as the Vinedresser. When we remain in an abiding or steadfast relationship with Christ, the fruit of the Spirit will be displayed in our lives. If we don't abide in Christ or, if Christ does not abide in us, we will not be able to display the fruit of the Holy Spirit.

What happens when a branch is cut from a tree? It withers and dies. As long as there is a connection, there is life. If you have a lamp and the light bulb works, but it is not plugged in, will the lamp light up? No, the lamp has to be connected. We, too, if we are not connected with Jesus, will not be able to walk in the fruit of the Spirit.

The Pruning Process

As the Vinedresser, the Father prunes us. Pruning means snipping away the dead twigs and branches because they are sucking the life out of the plant. When God prunes us, He takes away the dead things in our life so they won't start sucking the life out of us, too. Painful as it is, it is necessary – but know that the tree can grow bigger and stronger in the end.

Once pruned we, too, can demonstrate a changed life. People will look at us and immediately see the difference. Now you walk with a new confidence. When you know who you are in Christ, you will have a humble strength about you. You are not timid in front of people – though you are humble in the Lord. You are not holding back because you know your identity in Christ. You know that Christ has called you, and you want to stand up and be everything that He has called you to be.

Renewing our Mind

In verse 3 in the same passage Jesus says, *"You are already clean because of the word which I have spoken to you."* Yes, we are already washed by the blood of the Lamb and by the word of our testimony. We remain clean if we continue to abide in the word and choose to renew our mind. We do this when we stop agreeing with the world's way of thinking and get in line with God's thoughts. Even if the world's beliefs are legal, we still have to judge them according to the word, because nowadays a lot of this foolishness has become legal (and you know what I mean).

So if something in the world's system doesn't line up with the word of God, reject it. The Bible tells us not to be conformed to the patterns of this world but be transformed by the renewing of our mind (see Romans 12:2). We choose to have the mind of Christ (see 1 Corinthians 2:16). And walking in the fruit of the Spirit and being washed are part of the process of renewing our mind, washing out thoughts that defile and beginning to think differently.

Thinking differently can translate into being in the right place at the right time. This may involve moving to a new situation and being around different people who can help us move to the next level. You've heard the definition of insanity: doing the same things over and over again and expecting different results. Doing the same thing will surely produce the same results and you will still be in the same place this time next year – unsuccessful. If you want something different, you will have to do something different.

Jesus continues the vine analogy with these assuring words: *"**Abide** in **me** – **Hold fast** faith and a **good conscience**; and **let no trials turn you** aside from the **truth**"* (John 15:4 NIV, emphasis added). Yes, we will have trials and tribulations, but the Bible tells us that God has delivered us out of them all (see Psalm 34:19-20). Not some, but ALL. And know that, when trials and tribulations come, it is to teach us an important lesson right there.

Remember, if you take a test in God and fail, you are going to have to go around that mountain, get back on the other side and take that test again. And again … until you get it right. So if I were you, I would pay attention. My grandmother use to say, "Either you gonna pay cash or you gonna pay attention. Which one you wanna pay?" I use to be speeding all the time and get tickets. I am through with paying cash, so now I pay attention (I have slowed down).

As we allow the fruit of the Spirit, which is the character of Christ, to become our character, we slowly begin to change in the way we view circumstances. We now see them through the eyes of the Holy Spirit that's inside of us. We don't think, talk or believe the way we used to because our minds are being renewed. Isn't it true that the more you hang around a person in the natural, the more you begin to act, talk and walk and sound like them? If they have a favorite expression, before long you're using that, too. We are influenced by what we allow ourselves to be exposed to. So let's be intentional about exposing ourselves to God-fearing, genuine people of God.

Warning! This is a Public Service Announcement! Not everybody you think is abiding in Christ is totally renewed because we all have an under construction area that God is still working on. When it comes to our walk with Christ, the Bible says love covers a multitude of sin. Covering your brothers and sisters in prayer sometimes may require that you have a heart conversation with them to point out an area of weakness. Always be led by the Holy Spirit and do it in love.

GENTLENESS

The eighth fruit is gentleness. Gentleness is also translated into meekness – not weakness, but meekness. Gentleness is the quality of being kind, tender, or mild-mannered. Ephesians 4:32 tells us: *"... be kind to one another, tenderhearted, forgiving one another, even as God in Christ forgave you."*

Gentleness can be described as **power under control**. I may have the power to do various things but I choose to do it in a spirit of gentleness. I don't want to be brash. I don't want the love of power to overtake me. When I am walking in gentleness, I am allowing the Holy Spirit to bring that power under His control. You know, a lot of times when people are control freaks, they show that they don't trust anyone to get it right. But the fruit of gentleness places our strength under God's mighty hand and then it becomes a powerful tool.

Gentleness is most often displayed in our words, and words are powerful weapons. We can speak words of life or death over people or situations (see Proverbs 18:21). Gentleness constrains and channels that power so that we are bold enough to speak life to our mountains of difficulty till they are removed (see Mark 11:23).

There are many influences that direct our path. What are our major influences? For many, it's the marketplace and the media. These shape our perceptions by constant exposure to sin and the distortion of reality. Unconsciously, we become vulnerable to mainstream opinion and often blindly follow the crowd. But God's ways and thoughts are higher than those of the most enlightened experts in our institutions (see Isaiah 55:9). Let us not allow ourselves to be snared and confused by the babble of voices in the marketplace but let us tune in to the voice of the Holy Spirit directing our path:

> *Your own ears will hear him. Right behind you a voice will say, "This is the way you should go," whether to the right or to the left* (Isaiah 30:21 NLT).

Remember, God does want us to produce fruit, but He doesn't want it to be tainted. Let your fruit to be pure and genuine to reflect His very nature.

Gentleness to Confront

Gentleness, on the other hand, does not mean turning a blind eye to public sin. We tend to think gentleness means to go easy on people and try to excuse actions that God has called sin. Often we let someone be comfortable in their sin without speaking the truth because "It's none of my business – let the Holy Spirit deal with them!" That's being politically correct. But is it the will of God? We need to accept God's judgment on people and issues.

Paul tells us, "*… if a man should be caught in some trespass, you the spiritual ones restore such a one in a spirit of gentleness, considering yourself, lest you also be tempted*" (Galatians 6:1 Berean Literal Bible).

This doesn't mean being so soft that the sinner doesn't realize his wrong. It means confronting the brother or sister in a manner that is in line with scripture – mild, loving, encouraging, but also uncompromising about the holiness of God. Remember that our aim is not to condemn anyone but to restore that person in a spirit of love. Say to them, "I want to tell you something in love. I'm not telling you this to hurt your feelings but to help you to grow."

SELF-CONTROL

The last characteristic listed in Galatians 5:22-23 is self-control or temperance. This is, of course, the ability to control one's emotions. It involves moderation, constraint, and the ability to say "No" to ungodly desires and fleshly lusts such as rage, sexual appetites (including pornography), gossip, slander, lying, cheating. It also means restraint when we are tempted to become excessively emotional. When people see the outward change in our behavior from, say, a contentious, divisive person to one who watches his tongue and speaks good of others, or someone with a drinking habit who is now sober, they will surely recognize the hand of God.

Philippians 2:13 says "*… it is God who is at work in you, both to will and to work for His good pleasure.*" This transformation of our character is the fruit of the Spirit's work in our lives. We cannot acquire self-control through sheer will power. It is the Holy Spirit who develops it in us when we yield our mind and body to His cleansing work. Give God all the glory for this!

In this learning process, God is very gracious and deals with us according to our growth stage. He usually makes it easier on new believers but raises the bar for mature Christians. A friend of mine confided that as a new Christian she knew she had to quit smoking. But the habit was difficult to shake off because she had done it for so long. One night she asked the Holy Spirit to take it away. "Holy Spirit, I don't know how to pray this, but I ask You to take away all desire to smoke, in the name of Jesus. Not gradually but by tomorrow because I want my husband to see that Jesus is real ... and, Holy Spirit, You know how weak I am, so please completely remove the urge to smoke!" Know what? When she woke up the next day, she looked at the cigarette stubs in the ash tray and threw them all away. She never had any taste for cigarettes ever again! That was God!

Many months later, she asked the Holy Spirit for another favor. This time it was to take away her quick temper, which she had from childhood. But this time the Holy Spirit said, "You will have to work it out with me and develop self control!" It took months before she saw any change – but finally the temper was gone.

My story is about how God delivered me from the desire to smoke marijuana. God is not going to take away the things we enjoy just like that. We ourselves have to lay them down and turn them over to God, especially stuff we like. For me, my drug of choice was smoking weed ... I smoked it on and off for about fifteen years. I would tell myself this was the last time. I would throw it all out – the lighter, the paper, the weed – only to get up the next day and dig it all out of the trash again without truly wanting to be delivered. It was only when I continuously petitioned God to help me that I was able to make a conscious decision not to go around people that would be smoking marijuana (like some of my family members). Whenever I went to my brother's house, I would stay in the car and blow the horn and have them come out to the car because I knew that they were going to be in the house smoking weed.

So when it comes to self-control it's important for us to put up the boundaries so we won't be tempted. The Bible says that there's no temptation known to man for which God has not already made a way of escape. If there is something that you're tempted to do, I would say, yes, practice self-control. But, most of all, lay it down, give it to God so He can help you be delivered from anything that will cause you – or others – to stumble ... people are always watching us and the first thing they're going to say is, "I thought that you were supposed to be a Christian!"

What the issues you are struggling with? Anger, fear, substance addiction, pornography, backbiting, a critical attitude, emotional blackmail, laziness, negative self-talk? As a young dating couple, is sexual gratification a major issue? As a teen, are your friends putting pressure on you to give up reading the Bible? Nothing is too difficult for the Lord. But you must come to Him with the resolve to be rid of that habit because it is blocking your relationship with Him. Come before the Lord with all sincerity and ask Him for His mercy and grace to help. Ask the Holy Spirit to grow the fruit of self-control within you. He will not deny you because you asked in faith.

> *"[Not in your own strength] for it is God Who is all the while effectually at work in you [energizing and creating in you the power and desire], both to will and to work for His good pleasure and satisfaction and delight"* (Philippians 2:13 AMP).

Let's look at the ways we can cultivate good habits as we read further.

Chapter 6

CULTIVATING GOOD HABITS

As we grow in the fruit of the Spirit we are naturally adopting good habits and relinquishing the bad ones. One day, while I was studying about the fruit of self-control, I came across this poem on the internet.

WHO AM I ???

I am your constant companion.
I am your greatest helper or your heaviest burden.
I will push you onward or drag you down to failure.
I am completely at your command.
Half the things you do, you might just as well turn over to me,
and I will be able to do them quickly and correctly.
I am easily managed; you must merely be firm with me.
Show me exactly how you want something done, and after a few lessons I will do it automatically.

I am the servant of all great men.
And, alas, of all failures as well.
Those who are great, I have made great.
Those who are failures, I have made failures.
I am not a machine, though I work with all the precision of a machine.
Plus, the intelligence of a man.
You may run me for profit, or run me for ruin; it makes no difference to me.

> Take me, train me, be firm with me and I will put the world at your feet.
>
> Be easy with me, and I will destroy you.
>
> Who am I? I am a HABIT!

When 95% of people hear the word "habit," a negative thought pops up in their heads. Typically, most people think of a habit as being negative. The secret to your future lies in your daily habits, so ask yourself right now, "Are my habits today going to help me achieve my destiny?"

What are habits? They are actions we perform automatically without even thinking, like brushing your teeth in the morning, or driving to work. You don't have to concentrate on what you are doing because your mind is on auto-pilot, so to speak. When an action becomes a habit, it becomes ingrained in you. It becomes natural and spontaneous, like driving, because of continuous repetition. You can do it with skill and precision without thinking.

We can cultivate good habits in our daily routine by doing things that benefit ourselves and the people around us. For example, we could structure our lives in an orderly fashion: getting up at 6.00am, spending time in prayer, having breakfast, going to work/school, preparing dinner in the evening, taking the dog for a walk and interacting with the family, watching the news on TV before reading the word, and then going to bed.

But see how the balance gets upset when we don't exert discipline. You watched the late-night movie and couldn't get up when the alarm rang. There's no time for prayer, you're late for work, late home because work was unfinished, you had leftovers for dinner, the dog was not walked, you watched TV all night and fell asleep on the couch. If you were to continue in this haphazard pattern, bad habits would take over and make you unproductive.

In our digital culture, the social media induce many bad habits, especially for the young. Not only do you spend an excessive amount of time seeing what your "friends" on Facebook and Twitter are up to, your homework and chores suffer, and your conversations with family members are reduced to grunts. What's more you find yourself having to compromise on your values in order to gain acceptance from your peers. Who's in charge? You or the social media chat?

You might have to ask yourself what habits are pulling you down. I invite you to check out this list. Examine yourself and be honest about it:

Negativity

Am I Negative Nancy? No matter what it is, the glass is half empty.
Do I associate with negative people?
Am I a perpetual Worrier?
Do I walk in fear of what may happen? Remember that fear has torment (see 1 John 4:18).

Compromise

Do I avoid confrontation … because I want peace?
Do I hold back my own opinion because of the fear of what others may think?
Do I express different opinions in front of different audiences?
Am I double-minded, saying one thing and thinking another?
Am I silent when I have to defend the gospel?

Impatience

Do I dash as the light changes to red or honk when someone is too slow?
Do I have the habit of jumping to conclusions?
… or cutting in when someone is speaking?
… or finishing people's sentences?
Do I make an important decision hastily without waiting on the Lord?

Prejudice

Do I tend to prejudge people because I don't like their voice/color/gender/status/manner?

Do I echo the biases of my favorite news channel without checking with other sources?

Do I condemn a person or ministry because I do not agree with some of their teachings?

Procrastination

Do I have the habit of putting everything off till things pile up?
Am I late on my bills? It's not a money problem … it's a mind problem.
Do I start things and not finish … because something else got in the way?
Am I lazy?? Do I waste time on the web or network buzz?

Have I planned to read a book in the bible but never got round to it?

Control

Do I have the habit of control? Don't tell me I'm a control freak! … I've always had my way from young!

Do I pray soulish prayers – asking God to make people do what I want?

Taking offense

Am I usually defensive when criticized, rather than examine myself?
Do I have the habit of shifting the blame on to others rather than holding myself accountable?

Am I easily offended? Argumentative? Critical and judgmental?

Resisting change

Do I want everything to stay the way it is … it's much more comfortable?
Do I want to do it – my way?

Do I reminisce about the onions and leeks of my old life, not fully appreciating the pruning work of the Vinedresser in my new life?

How did you fare, especially with the last point in each category? If you did rather well, congratulations! But most of us need to examine our own hearts.

If we think our bad habit is not a big deal, the bible says it is the "little foxes" that spoil the vine (see Song of Solomon 2:15). That "white lie" you told your spouse, that extra change given by the cashier you quietly slipped into your pocket may look like small things but ... think about it. Are you not sowing into the spirit of lying and cheating? Guard your heart! These things done unconsciously can add up to an attitude that breeds a complacent and lukewarm spirit ... and that is something God hates.

Bad habits will delay, detour or even block you from your destiny .... If you know it is something you want to do or something God is calling you to do, it is your responsibility to prepare for where you are going. Your habits can make you or break you. When opportunity comes knocking, you can't start getting ready: you have to be ready, and being ready means cultivating the habits that will prepare you for YOUR NEXT! Whatever your next may be!!

One bad habit is to compare ourselves with others. We are all unique and have different gifts and talents ...If we constantly think others are better than us in every way, then we undermine yourself.

Another is to think running away from Confrontation is not a bad thing. But you can't keep running away from challenging conditions. No matter what you do, you will, at some point and time in your life, find yourself in middle of a hard and sometime depressing condition which is, by nature, very challenging.

How do I break my bad habits?

First of all, come to God with a broken and humble heart and ask for His help.

> *The sacrifices of God are a broken spirit,*
> *A broken and a contrite heart—*
> *These, O God, You will not despise* (Psalm 51:17).

*"God resists the proud,
But gives grace to the humble."
   Therefore submit to God. Resist the devil and he will flee from you.   Draw near to God and He will draw near to you* (James 4:6-7).

1. **Start Now ….**

Don't wait. NOW is the time to create new habits.

Do not boast about tomorrow, for you do not know what a day may bring forth (Proverbs 27:1).

Don't plan projects based on "Someday I'll do …" waiting for the perfect conditions.

*He who observes the wind will not sow, and he who regards the clouds will not reap (*Ecclesiastes 11:4).

"One of these days" is "none of these days!"

2. **Own it – be personally accountable**

Many of us refuse to blame ourselves for where we are. It's always easier to excuse ourselves and blame others. It's all Excuse and Accuse …. "It's my Momma's fault; she never taught me to _____!" "It's my Daddy! He set a bad example by _____!" "It's God's fault! Why did He have to let that happen to me?"

After all, THE BLAME GAME is as old as the Garden!

Adam: "The woman, the woman you gave me, she made me do it!"

Eve   : "The snake lied to me! I was ignorant!"

And the snake? "I couldn't help it! That's my nature!"

God gave us free will and the grace to overcome but we succumbed to our flesh. If you really want to change and be free, the first step is to OWN IT and don't twist it.

The foolishness of a man twists his way,

And his heart frets against the Lord (Proverbs 19:3).

So today, I **decree and declare** that I am coming out of foolishness to make better choices.

3. **Do an internal audit**

    Take stock of your bad habits. Where am I tempted? What do I need to improve? Who do I need to forgive?

    Test yourself … evaluate yourself … take a real hard look at yourself.

    Then ask yourself: "What are my strengths? What are my weaknesses?"

    "What are my triggers?"

    "Why can't I be on time?"

    "Why am I a compulsive shopper?"

    "How can I plan better for the next day?"

    "What areas of my life am I lazy in?"

    "What areas am I coasting in?" Remember, if you are coasting, you are really going downhill!

    "What does God want me to do in this season?"

    "How can I prepare for the next season?"

4. **Avoid places of temptation**

    These include bars and night clubs, certain websites, certain neighborhoods etc.

    Remember the young man caught by the harlot?

    Passing along the street near her corner;
    *And **he took the path** to her house …*
    And there a woman met him,

With the attire of a harlot, and a crafty heart …
(Proverbs 7:8,10)

Notice how he intentionally took the street that led to her house and immediately got snared when she accosted him.

5. **Avoid the company of gossips**

   My Grandmother use to say, "A dog who brings a bone, will carry a bone." If a person is talking about other people and telling you their business, you'd BETTER believe that same person will be telling your business and talking about you to others, too.

   The words of a talebearer are like tasty trifles, and they go down into the inmost body (Proverbs 18:8).

   When you sit down to a meal with them, you are off-guard and literally take in their gossip spirit with their juicy snippets.

6. **Stop your own loose talk**

   You are snared by the words of your mouth; You are taken by the words of your mouth (Proverbs 6:2).

   The Bible discourages using a lot of words where a few would suffice. "*Even fools are thought wise if they keep silent, and discerning if they hold their tongues*" (Proverbs 17:28 NIV). Those who feel compelled to express every thought in their heads usually end up in trouble. Modern society offers many platforms to express ourselves verbally. Social media, blogs, cell phones, and call-in radio all give us the ability to keep up a constant stream of chit-chatting. But how much of all that talking is truly edifying or important (see Ephesians 4:29)? Saying what needs to be said is important, but talking too much easily leads to saying things that should not be said.

7. **Find an Accountability Partner**

   Find someone who can keep confidences and can support you with prayer and firm counsel.

*Though one may be overpowered by another, two can withstand him. And a **threefold cord** is not quickly broken* (Ecclesiastes 4:12).

Who forms the third cord? Jesus. Did He not say?

"For where two or three are gathered together in My name, I am there in the midst of them" (Matthew 18:20).

Your Accountability Partner will help course correct you along the way.

8. **Give Him all the glory!**

   Our words have the power to destroy and the power to build up. Let's be mindful of our words (see Proverbs 12:6). The writer of Proverb tells us, *"The tongue has the power of life and death, and those who love it will eat its frui*t" (Proverbs 18:21 NIV). How are we using our words?? Are we using them to build up people or destroy them? Are they filled with hate or love, bitterness or blessing, complaining or compliments, lust or love, victory or defeat?

   When we consider the reasons why we should praise God, we find a list of His attributes. He is full of glory (see Psalm 138:5), great (see Psalm 145:3), wise and powerful (see Daniel 2:20), good (see Psalm 107:8), merciful and faithful (see Psalm 89:1), and much more. This list of attributes is complemented by a list of His wonderful works. He is the One who saves us (see Psalm 18:46), keeps His promises (see 1 Kings 8:56), pardons sin (see Psalm 103:1-3), and gives us our daily food (see Psalm 136:25). To try to list all the things God has done is impossible, but it is a wonderful exercise because it turns our hearts back to Him and keeps us mindful of how much we owe to Him.

   Illustrations of victories from people who cultivated good habits apply to us too!

*"Train up a child in the way he should go,
And when he is old he will not depart from it"* (Proverbs 22:6)

Daniel's habit of praying at set times in the same place made it easier to resist the command of Darius.

Good habits pay off. For instance, I have a habit of completing what I start out to do. I know it may sound simple but a lot of people start things and never complete them. Also, I really try to be a woman of my word. If I say I'm going to do something, I do everything in my power to do it. (My father taught me to do what you say, and mean what you say.) Even if, for some reason something comes up and I will not be able to do it, I will try to let the person know as soon as I can.

Cultivating good habits it helps put you in the mindset of having good results, so a good habit is to have my prayer time every morning. Another good habit is to smile and say "Please" and "Thank you." These are simple things that my parents taught me but I find that they open up doors for me and help me to get opportunities. Another good habit is to always have a heart of gratitude – to be thankful for where you are, who you are, what you are, what God has given you. A lot of times I think people focus on what they don't have instead of focusing on what they do have and appreciating what they do have. Cultivating good habits will just keep you getting good results.

The Character to be a Witness

God wants to mold our character so that we can go from glory to glory. As our habits change, our very thought life begins to change. Our vision is enlarged and we can make His priorities our priorities. Let's allow the Holy Spirit to take control of our life. Jesus promised that we would never be alone but the Holy Spirit is with us to be our constant Guide, Teacher, Seal of salvation, and Comforter (see John 14:16-18).

I know I've said this before but I want to remind us all again that God wants us to be true and faithful witnesses of the gospel wherever we go. It is the Holy Spirit's power that would help us develop the character to represent Jesus:

> *"But you will receive power **when the Holy Spirit comes on you**; and you will be my witnesses in Jerusalem, and in all Judea and Samaria, and to the ends of the earth"* (Acts 1:8).

The salvation of souls is such an awesome supernatural work and we are privileged to be the ministers of it. We can only carry out this function when we yield ourselves as vessels so that the anointing of the Holy Spirit can flow through us. God wants to give you the power to witness the word. Can He trust you with the power to be a strong witness for Christ not only in your preaching but in your daily habits? Can you give Him all the Glory!

Chapter 7

BREAKING GENERATIONAL CURSES

I'm sure by now you can't wait to get to the gifts of the Holy Spirit. But before we do that, I sense in my spirit the need to deal with issues that seem like a wall blocking us from the blessings that God has destined for us. Specifically, I want to deal with generational curses. I sense that this is the NOW time to break any lingering generational curses over your life today! Hallelujah! I decree and declare that, as you read and grasp this message, every generational curse will be broken off you by the power of God!

This message also comes with important instructions on how to break generational curses off your bloodline. Only then will you, your children, your grandchildren and great-grandchildren be free to walk in the blessings of God ... for a thousand generations (see Exodus 20:6).

Let's first understand Jesus' Mission statement when He came down to earth: What He came to accomplish, and then His Vision: How He would accomplish it.

Jesus' Mission Statement: to destroy the works of the devil

> *Little children, let no one deceive you. He who practices righteousness is righteous, just as He is righteous. He who sins is of the devil, for the devil has sinned from the beginning.* **For this purpose the Son of God was manifested, that He might destroy the works of the devil.** *Whoever has been born of God does not sin, for His seed remains in him; and he cannot sin, because he has been born of God* (1 John 3:7-9).

" *... that He may destroy the works of the devil.*" Generational curses are the works of the devil and Jesus came to break generational curses.

Jesus' Vision Statement: to release blessings on us

The thief does not come except to steal, and to kill, and to destroy. I have come that they may have life, and that they may have it more abundantly (**John 10:10**).

Jesus came to give us a life of abundance. God's gift of Jesus is not just about your going to heaven: it's about the Kingdom. Jesus wants to shine through your life so you can show forth His glory, so you can attract people and point them to the Kingdom. It's about you receiving the blessing and living a life full to the overflow with nothing broken, nothing missing.

The Full Benefits of the Cross

You see, salvation is both a one-time decision as well as a process. The word "salvation" comes from the Greek word *soteria* meaning "deliverance." When we give our life to Jesus for the first time, we are delivered from the ownership of satan. Salvation is also a continuous process of being set free from our old sinful nature as we yield to the mighty hand of God. Again, salvation provides for our healing by the wounds of Jesus on the cross (see Isaiah 53:5). Salvation also provides "escapes from death" (see Psalm 68:20), and this includes the breaking of curses. Old cycles or generational curses can be destroyed and new cycles or generational blessings released.

What are Generational Curses?

Generational curses are the effects of our ancestors' sins. If not repented of and renounced, they are passed down our bloodline from generation to generation. Let me illustrate. Your mamma never got married and had a child out of wedlock, and your aunty had a child out of wedlock, then you had a baby out of wedlock, then your daughter has a child out of wedlock. Nine times out of ten that's a generational curse.

If great granddaddy was an alcoholic, and if daddy drank heavily, your brother is addicted to cigarettes and your nephew is addicted to gambling, that's a generational curse, too. We also need to recognize that if Daddy was a "rolling stone" (wherever he laid his head was his home), if your papa was a rolling stone, and your brother is a rolling stone, and your nephew is hooked on pornography, nine times out of ten that's a generational curse.

The word of God mentions "generational curses" in several places (see Exodus 20:5; 34:7; Numbers 14:18; Deuteronomy 5:9). God cautions that He is *"a jealous God, punishing the children for the sin of the fathers to the third and fourth generation of those who hate me"* (Exodus 20:5 NIV).

The antidote to a generational curse is repentance. When Israel turned from idols to serve the living God, the "curse" was broken and God saved them (see Judges 3:9, 15; 1 Samuel 12:10-11). Yes, God promised to visit Israel's sin upon the third and fourth generations, but in the very next verse He promised that He would show *"love to a thousand generations of those who love me and keep my commandments"* (Exodus 20:6 BSB). For someone worried about a generational curse, the answer is salvation through Jesus Christ. A Christian is a new creation (see 2 Corinthians 5:17).

The Divine Exchange

So we don't have to remain under generational curses any longer. When Jesus went to the cross for us, He took on everything that was accursed so that we could walk in blessing. He became rejection, He became lust, He became death, He became sickness in our place.

> *Christ has redeemed us from the curse of the law, having become a curse for us (for it is written, "Cursed is everyone who hangs on a tree") that the blessing of*

Abraham might come upon the Gentiles in Christ Jesus, that we might receive the promise of the Spirit through faith (Galatians 3:13-14).

You see, at the cross a divine exchange took place. Jesus exchanged the curses due to us for the blessings of the cross. The blood of Jesus canceled every generational curse – **EVERYTHING** – spiritually, physically, mentally, financially, emotionally, and exchanged it for His blessing. He died that we may have life – not just any kind of life but life to the fullest. So check yourself. If your new life in Christ is not vastly superior to your former life, chances are you have not started to unwrap the GIFT through knowing Him.

The Blessing of Abraham

Christ became a curse for all the sins of mankind, past, present and future, so that the blessing of Abraham might be ours. As the spiritual seed of Abraham through Christ, we, too, inherit the promises of Abraham. Here are the blessings of Abraham we can claim:

> *"Now it shall come to pass, if you diligently obey the voice of the LORD your God, to observe carefully all His commandments which I command you today, that the LORD your God will set you high above all nations of the earth. And all these blessings shall come upon you and overtake you, because you obey the voice of the LORD your God:*
>
> *"Blessed shall you be in the city, and blessed shall you be in the country.*
>
> *"Blessed shall be the fruit of your body, the produce of your ground and the increase of your herds, the increase of your cattle and the offspring of your flocks.*
>
> *"Blessed shall be your basket and your kneading bowl.*

"Blessed shall you be when you come in, and blessed shall you be when you go out.

"The LORD will cause your enemies who rise against you to be defeated before your face; they shall come out against you one way and flee before you seven ways.

"The LORD will command the blessing on you in your storehouses and in all to which you set your hand, and He will bless you in the land which the LORD your God is giving you.

"The LORD will establish you as a holy people to Himself, just as He has sworn to you, if you keep the commandments of the LORD your God and walk in His ways. Then all peoples of the earth shall see that you are called by the name of the LORD, and they shall be afraid of you. And the LORD will grant you plenty of goods, in the fruit of your body, in the increase of your livestock, and in the produce of your ground, in the land of which the LORD swore to your fathers to give you. The LORD will open to you His good treasure, the heavens, to give the rain to your land in its season, and to bless all the work of your hand. You shall lend to many nations, but you shall not borrow. And the LORD will make you the head and not the tail; you shall be above only, and not be beneath, if you heed the commandments of the LORD your God, which I command you today, and are careful to observe them. So you shall not turn aside from any of the words which I command you this day, to the right or the left, to go after other gods to serve them (Deuteronomy 28:1-14).

    But there is one condition: we must diligently obey the voice of the LORD your God, to observe carefully all His commandments (see

Deuteronomy 28:1).

Understand that blessing is not just about a house, car, job or mate. Blessing is being empowered to succeed, *"for it is He who gives you power to get wealth that He may establish His covenant which He swore to your fathers ..."* (Deuteronomy 8:18).

If you live in the United States of America, you are blessed. Even if you're in a poor neighborhood, out of work, or on government assistance, you have blessings people in other countries would love to trade with you. Think about everything that God has given you, all the blessings He has poured out, material, physical, social or spiritual. Most of us have far more than we really understand. Compared to the world's truly poor, I am wealthy beyond belief, and you probably are, too.

God's Riches at Christ's Expense (GRACE)

All generational curses are broken by the blood of Jesus and we receive grace by divine exchange: **Grace** – "**G**od's Riches **A**t **C**hrist's **E**xpense!"

> He endured poverty so that we might have abundance (see 2 Corinthians 8:9).
>
> He bore our shame that we might receive glory (see 2 Corinthians 5:21).
>
> He bore our rejection that we might be accepted by the Father (see Ephesians 1:6).
>
> The "old man" in us died that the "new man" could be resurrected (see Romans 6:6).

I'm going to call out some generational curses and you can also write down your own generational curses because we are going to renounce them today.

Poverty is a generational curse. Possessiveness is a generational curse. Sexual sin, mental illness, substance abuse, physical disease, mental and emotional illness, occult involvement, fear, anxiety, and anger, all of them are generational curses and under each label are other categories. But, today, I just want to lay a foundation about generational curses – so we can identify them and remove them from our lives.

What do you do when word curses are spoken over you? "You were not planned; you were an accident," "You are a jerk or a failure," "You are clumsy/stupid/good-for-nothing," "You are a slow learner," "You will never succeed."

Here's what you do:

> ONE, I acknowledge all word curses which have been spoken over me.
>
> TWO, I denounce each of these curses as lies from the enemy.
>
> THREE, I replace each word curse with the truth of God's Word.
>
> FOUR, I walk in a new way.
>
> For example:
>
> The curse: "You can't do anything right."
>
> The answer: "I can do all things through Christ who strengthens me (see Philippians 4:13). Therefore, I declare that I can do anything that is in the will of God."
>
> The curse: "You will never be able to afford a house!"
>
> The answer: "And my God shall supply all my need according to His riches in glory by Christ Jesus" (see Philippians 4:19).
>
> The curse: "You suffer from deep rejection. You will never recover."

The answer: "Christ was rejected so that I can be accepted (see Isaiah 53:3). Because Christ bore my rejection, I declare that I am accepted in the Beloved!" (see Ephesians 1:6).

Unwrap the Gift of Christ

We have established that Jesus came to destroy the works of the enemy. He came that we can walk in generational blessings. The only thing we have to do is unwrap the Gift of Christ and appropriate everything that God says we can have. Jesus gave us the Holy Spirit who brought us nine gifts. So, whether you are imparting or receiving the Gifts, be very sensitive to the leading of the Holy Spirit. As Mary said at the marriage feast, "Do what He says!"

So if you want to operate in the gifts, you have only to ask the Holy Spirit for the particular gifts you desire. Ask Him to bless you with the anointing to walk in them. At the same time, understand that it is His prerogative to give to whosoever He pleases: *"But one and the same Spirit works all these things, distributing to each one individually as He wills"* (1 Corinthians 12:11). Because our God is sovereign!

Chapter 8

THE GIFTS OF THE SPIRIT -THE GIFTS THAT KNOW SOMETHING: THE REVELATION GIFTS-

We are now going to look at the nine Gifts of the Holy Spirit in general and the first three Revelation Gifts in particular. The word "gifts" in this context is derived from the Greek word *pneumatikos* meaning "spiritual." These are spiritual gifts freely give to us by God, in demonstration of the His power: *"'Not by might nor by power, but by My Spirit,' says the LORD of hosts"* (Zechariah 4:6). We cannot earn our gifts or mimic them in our own human way. But we can learn to cooperate with the Holy Spirit by desiring them and being willing channels for the release of the gifts.

Let us begin by having a clear understanding of all the gifts.

First, we need to know that God the Father, the Son Jesus and Holy Spirit have each given us distinct gifts and we should learn to clearly differentiate them. These gifts show the **Trinity at work in different ways to enable us to be effective in our life and calling.**

The Father who Energizes: the Grace gifts

For I say, through the grace given to me, to everyone who is among you, not to think of himself more highly

> *than he ought to think, but to think soberly, as God has dealt to each one a measure of faith. For as we have many members in one body, but all the members do not have the same function, so we, being many, are one body in Christ, and individually members of one another. Having then gifts differing according to the grace that is given to us, let us use them: if prophecy, let us prophesy in proportion to our faith; or ministry, let us use it in our ministering; he who teaches, in teaching; he who exhorts, in exhortation; he who gives, with liberality; he who leads, with diligence; he who shows mercy, with cheerfulness* (Romans 12:3-8).

Although the body of Christ has many members, the Father has created each one of us as a unique individual. Each of us is endowed us with seven basic traits or inclinations towards any of the following: prophecy, ministry, teaching, exhortation, giving, leading and showing mercy. He has also given each of us a certain measure of faith through which we can activate the grace gifts needed to move in those inclinations. How much we stir up that particular grace gift of the Father will help us to be effective in our calling.

We see how Barnabas stirred up his ministry gifting by being a generous giver. But by Acts 13:2 God had promoted him to apostle: "*Now separate to Me Barnabas and Saul for the work to which I have called them.*" In the days of the early church, Stephen and Philip stirred up their gifting by serving at tables the best way they could. Shortly after, they were seen preaching the word with anointing and performing miracles (Acts 6:8-10; 8:5-8).

The Lord Jesus who Administrates: the Five-Fold Ministry

> *And He Himself gave some to be apostles, some prophets, some evangelists, and some pastors and teachers, for the equipping of the saints for the work of*

> *ministry, for the edifying of the body of Christ, till we all come to the unity of the faith and of the knowledge of the Son of God, to a perfect man, to the measure of the stature of the fullness of Christ; that we should no longer be children, tossed to and fro and carried about with every wind of doctrine, by the trickery of men, in the cunning craftiness of deceitful plotting, but, speaking the truth in love, may grow up in all things into Him who is the head—Christ* (Ephesians 4:11-15).

Jesus Christ has appointed leaders to help build up the body of Christ and to help us grow up in all things. This is known as the five-fold ministry. It consists of apostles, prophets, evangelists, pastors and teachers – and various combinations of them, for example, prophet-teacher, apostle-prophet, pastor-evangelist and many more. You see, the Father first defines you, and then Jesus gives you ministry gifts to equip you for what you can become.

The gifts of ministry were imparted to the young Timothy by Paul when he ordained him pastor of the church at Ephesus. (He likely laid hands on him on other occasions, too.) Here Paul is encouraging Timothy to keep the fire burning by stirring it up on his own. He was to remain fervent in the gifts and not allow his spirit to be discouraged even though Paul was now in prison.

> *Therefore I remind you to stir up the gift of God which is in you through the laying on of my hands. For God has not given us a spirit of fear, but of power and of love and of a sound mind* (2 Timothy 1:6-7).

What were the particular gifts of ministry were imparted here? Fearlessness, power, love, and a sound mind because that is what Timothy needed most under his trying circumstances.

The Holy Spirit who Enables: Gifts of the Holy Spirit

> *There are diversities of gifts, but the same Spirit. There are differences of ministries, but the same Lord. And*

> *there are diversities of activities, but it is the same God who works all in all. But the manifestation of the Spirit is given to each one for the profit of all: for to one is given the word of wisdom through the Spirit, to another the word of knowledge through the same Spirit, to another faith by the same Spirit, to another gifts of healings by the same Spirit, to another the working of miracles, to another prophecy, to another discerning of spirits, to another different kinds of tongues, to another the interpretation of tongues. But one and the same Spirit works all these things, distributing to each one individually as He wills* (1 Corinthians 12:4-11).

So the Father tells you what He created you to be. Jesus places five-fold ministers in His Church to help you become effective in your calling, and the Holy Spirit enables you to fulfill your ministry potential with His gifts.

The important thing to emphasize is the unity of the Body of Christ in the midst of these giftings. There are diversities of gifts, but the same Holy Spirit. There are differences of ministries, but the same Lord. And there are diverse activities, but the same God who works in all.

Many members but unity in one body

The Body of Christ consists of different pieces jointly knit together for the profit of all. God works in each individual to benefit the whole body. As you share your gifts, all can profit.

Diversity of ministries but the same spirit

The diversity of ministries points to your ministry fingerprint. Are you asked to lead a home fellowship? Pastor a mega church? Are you called into street evangelism, or TV ministry? Are you called into specific nations? Are you a giver like Barnabas to support the sent-out ones?

Diversity of gifts and activity but it's the same God

We are gifted differently but God's work is unified. He will use us all to complement each other in the body of Christ. Some operate in the gifts of healings, some are anointed prophets, others are pastor-teachers. And just as they are important, we also need anointed servants of God to mow the lawn and clean the bathrooms! Hallelujah! We need watchmen on the walls, who are going to be praying in the Spirit and warning the church. We need a team of singers to lead worship in the house of the Lord. All of us come with our different gifts and activities but we honor the same God.

What the Gifts do

The gifts are tools that we use here on earth for the supernatural power of God to manifest so that His purposes are accomplished. The Holy Spirit distributes the gifts to whomever He wills and in whatever situation He wants you to use them.

In all things, God gets the glory. No one can take credit for getting anyone saved. It's the Holy Spirit. For *"no one can say that Jesus is Lord except by the Holy Spirit"* (1 Corinthians 12:3). What the gifts do is to proclaim Jesus Christ as Lord. It's not to glorify a person – it's always to point you to Jesus. Our identity is never to become absorbed in a gift, but in The Giver – Jesus Christ – and the ministry of the Holy Spirit in our lives.

So be Real in your Witness

So, whatever your activity, be real and transparent about yourself. Revelation 12:11 says, *"And they overcame him by the blood of the Lamb and by the word of their testimony, and they did not love their lives to the death."* We overcome by the blood of Jesus and the word of our testimony. If you have an uplifting story to share, it may be the thing that gets through to the one in desperate need. So if you were a drug dealer or you were on crack or committing sexually immoral sins, it's that testimony of how God delivered you that is going to bring hope to somebody else. God wants real people so that the lost can be pulled out of darkness and set on track.

When we present ourselves with a starchy and holier-than-thou front, people think that they can never live up to that. Some get turned off.

GIFTS OF THE HOLY SPIRIT

And now we come to the gifts of the Holy Spirit. There are nine of them and they come in three packages of three. Remember, three is the number for perfection.

There are the revelation gifts. They reveal something: the Word of Knowledge, the Word of Wisdom and the Discerning of Spirits.

Then there're the power gifts. They do something: the gift of Faith, the gift of Miracles and the gifts of Healings.

And, finally, there are the Inspiration gifts. They say something. They are the gift of Prophecy, the gift of Tongues and the gift of Interpretation of Tongues.

In this chapter we will focus on the Revelation gifts.

WORD OF KNOWLEDGE

This is when the Holy Spirit drops into your heart a specific word about someone or something that you would never have known under natural circumstances. The word of knowledge can come unexpectedly – when we are driving, or at the supermarket or at a church meeting. It may come as an audible word, a word in your head, or a vision. It may also be something you sense. It is generally a cue to pray or to act upon that knowledge.

An evangelist speaker I know usually waits upon the Lord to show him things even before the meeting begins. Usually the Holy Spirit's spotlight will pan the congregation and give him an "x-ray vision" of certain ones. It could be their skeletal frame, or a condition with one of their organs or their circulatory system. As he ministers and calls out the condition, the healing anointing flows and the person receives his healing.

We see another example of the word of knowledge in John 4. Here Jesus made a detour to Samaria because He already knew He was to meet this particular woman at the well. And there she was – alone. Jesus was able to open up a conversation with her and quickly steer it towards spiritual matters by talking about the fountain of living water. Then, without causing any offense, He used a very personal word of knowledge: that she had had five husbands and the one she was living with was not her husband. The woman was immediately able to perceive that He was a prophet.

Jesus was then able to deliver the full salvation message:

> *"Woman, believe Me, the hour is coming when you will neither on this mountain, nor in Jerusalem, worship the Father. You worship what you do not know; we know what we worship, for salvation is of the Jews. But the hour is coming, and now is, when the true worshipers will worship the Father in spirit and truth; for the Father is seeking such to worship Him. God is Spirit, and those who worship Him must worship in spirit and truth"* (John 4:21-25).

I read on CBN.com about a dramatic event where the word of knowledge came to an airplane pilot. The news channel reports that on September 28 2018, at the same time a powerful earthquake struck Indonesia, one plane managed to miraculously take off from the Palu airport, barely escaping the destruction.

Pilot Ricoseta Mafella, a devout Christian, said that moments before the earthquake and tsunami hit Indonesia, he felt the urge to sing aloud. "God seemed like He was saying, 'Hey, just praise me and worship me.'" Captain Mafella says he saw nothing unusual as he approached Palu that day. Then, as the passengers departed and Mafella prepared for his return flight, he says he heard God's voice instructing him, "Be quick, get out of this place. Depart early."

Mafella did not wait to hear more. He got permission from air traffic control to take off three minutes earlier than scheduled. Exactly 3 minutes after take-off, the town was hit by the highest 7.7 and 7.4 magnitude quakes ever! By leaving 3 minutes early his plane narrowly escaped the destruction caused by the strong tremors. "Those runway cracks are 2 meters deep. Behind, the runway had melted. They happened on my departure time!"he said.

WORD OF WISDOM

So we see, the word of knowledge presents us with raw facts or instructions in a given situation. But what do we do with it? Do not act independently but wait for the Holy Spirit to give you the next gift, which is the Word of Wisdom.

When you have the word of wisdom, you then have the big picture and know what to do. Through the word of knowledge, you may know, for instance, that a certain person is going through many challenges in his job and is thinking of quitting. These are the facts. Now the Holy Spirit reveals through the word of wisdom that there is a promotion round the corner and that he must not quit because the favor of the Lord is coming upon him.

Or you have the word of knowledge that the person is going through a painful marriage. Then the word of wisdom cautions you not to broadcast this matter so specifically but to couch it in more general terms. So you say publicly, "You are going through some challenges in your personal life. But the Lord is saying that He has heard your cries and will give you the grace to come through the fire. The outcome will be good." The woman who came seeking a solution is comforted and the congregation is edified.

A friend of mine tells me of the time she first went up for prayer as a new believer. "This was my first encounter with Holy Spirit gifts. I was pretty messed up. When it was my turn, the pastor prayed for me and he saw a cracked mirror with fragments of glass." She, too, had a vision of a frame with pieces of glass hanging on to it. As he spoke, she saw one large shard break off and fall to the ground. Clunk! She knew the past was over!

Then the pastor said something incredible! "But I see the Lord remaking the mirror as you surrender your life to him. And it's something beautiful!" Only the Holy Spirit knew those words would mean something so significant to her.

DISCERNING OF SPIRITS

The discerning of spirits must be distinguished from general discernment. General discernment is the ability to judge or sense things through your own natural ability. The Holy Spirit may guide you but it is not a gift. For example, you may be about to close a business deal but you sense that the person is not telling the truth. Maybe it's his body language or tone of voice. Or you suddenly have the urge to pray for someone, and later realize they were nearly involved in a collision with a truck. That's a prompting by the Holy Spirit but it's not the gift of discerning spirits.

The discerning of spirits has more to do with seeing into the spirit realm to know whether the spirits are of God or from the devil. This gift is vital for anyone involved in ministry, especially those engaged in spiritual warfare.

In Acts 16, we find Paul and Silas in Philippi confronted by a slave girl who practiced fortune telling for her owners. For many days she would follow them around, crying,

> *"These men are the servants of the Most High God, who proclaim to us the way of salvation." But Paul, greatly annoyed, turned and said to the spirit, "I command you*

in the name of Jesus Christ to come out of her.' And he came out that very hour" (Acts 16:17-18).

While what she was saying was true, Paul was able to discern the spirit of divination and did not need an evil spirit to advertise their ministry.

Warning about the laying on of hands

Earlier we saw Paul reminding Timothy about the gifts that were imparted to him by the laying on of hands (see 2 Timothy 1:6-7).

However in another situation, Paul warns Timothy not to lay hands too hastily on people.

Do not lay hands on anyone hastily, nor share in other people's sins; keep yourself pure (1 Timothy 5:22).

In other words, take care you do not appoint anyone to serve in the church without first testing their character. If you do and they are publicly sinning, then you are participating in that sin. Examine yourself, too, and keep yourself pure.

Paul goes on to say

Some men's sins are clearly evident, preceding them to judgment, but those of some men follow later. Likewise, the good works of some are clearly evident, and those that are otherwise cannot be hidden (1 Timothy 5:24-25).

We are not to be seen to be condoning the sins of another by recommending them to a leadership position in the church. We must keep ourselves pure. This is a sound advice for anyone thinking of serving or appointing anyone to serve in the church, for this is a sacred office.

This reminds me of a similar scripture in Isaiah which says:

*Depart! Depart! Go out from there,
Touch no unclean thing;*

> *Go out from the midst of her,*
> *Be clean,*
> *You who bear the vessels of the LORD* (Isaiah 52:11).

We who minister must make sure we walk in holiness because we bear the vessels of the Lord. You know, a lot of times, we see people with impressive gifts doing great miracles and attracting a lot of attention. Later, we find out that their lives are not holy – and I'm not talking about things like driving on when the traffic lights are red or not stopping at a stop sign! They are living in adultery, or they have issues with integrity or covetousness, or they backbite. Or they do not preach the gospel of Jesus Christ but another gospel: the hyper grace doctrine or the prosperity gospel without preaching repentance. The Grace of God covers a multitude of sins, but that does not give you a license to keep on SINNING.

We ask ourselves how it is still possible for such people to manifest the gifts? Well, look at "*…for God's gifts and his call are irrevocable*" (Romans 11:29 NIV): in other words, once a gift is given, it cannot be taken back.

My dear brothers and sisters, let us be sober and watchful. Let's not judge things by how they look. Let's judge things by character. God is saying, "It's not the gifts; it's the fruit of that person you need to be looking out for. When I say you'll know them by their fruit, you'll know my people by their character, and their character is the Fruit of The Spirit."

Look for Love

At the end of his discourse on the gifts of the Holy Spirit, Paul encourages us to "*earnestly desire the best gifts*" and continues with this amazing statement: "*… and yet I show you a more excellent way…*" (1 Corinthians 12:31). What is this more excellent way? Love. The whole of Chapter 13 goes on to talk about the quality of love. Love is a fruit. Though we might do the most impressive acts but lack love, he says we are nothing but *"a sounding brass or a clanging cymbal"* (verse 1).

Love means that this spiritual gift is not for me to hold on to. It's for me to deliver to someone else. When a gift is ministered in the spirit of love, it will be delivered in the most gracious manner. It will follow the example set by Jesus of how the word of knowledge, or healings and miracles function: with love and compassion. When the person being ministered to sees the spirit of love, he is more open to hearing what the Lord is saying and receiving his miracle.

Let us use our gifts in the right spirit. The gifts we display are meant to show forth the love of God for His people. If, however, we are more concerned about our performance rather than the very people God wants to touch, then we have missed the whole point. For, when the gifts from the throne room of God flow to others in the same spirit of love and compassion, this is the ultimate expression of the grace of God. At all times, we must guard our hearts and never give in to the spirit of pride and arrogance – that is another spirit. If you are gifted in a certain direction, simply give thanks to the Father, the Son and the Holy Spirit. There is no need to boast or feel superior.

We therefore realize that our spiritual gift is not a medal of honor. Rather, it is the tool God has given us to do supernatural things here on earth. We the body of Christ should desire these spiritual gifts every day of our lives. They should be in operation at every single service. What's more, they should be present in our daily lives, not just at church services. Whether we are at work, whether we're on the bus, whether we're in school, we should always be ready for that gift to be activated and we should be yielding to the Holy Spirit to use us in any way He sees fit. GLORY BE TO GOD!!!!!

Chapter 9

THE GIFTS OF THE SPIRIT
-THE GIFTS THAT DO SOMETHING:
THE POWER GIFTS-

In this chapter we are going to discuss the Power gifts or Gifts that do something. Are you now eager to receive the supernatural gifts that the Holy Spirit has for you?

THE POWER GIFTS

In Chapter 8 we looked at a foundational scripture, 1 Corinthians 12:1-14, in which Paul is describing the nine gifts of the Holy Spirit. We saw that these nine gifts fall into three categories:

The Revelation Gifts that Reveal something (We covered them in the last chapter.)

The Power Gifts that Do something

The Inspiration Gifts that Say something

In this chapter we will look at the Power Gifts, the gifts that do something. The Power Gifts are also known as Dynamic gifts based on the Greek word *dunamis* which suggests explosive power. The power gifts are Faith, Miracles and Healings.

Before we look at the Gift of Faith, I want to teach a little bit more about faith because there are several gifts of faith.

Faith for Salvation

First, there is faith for salvation. This is the faith to believe that Christ is the Son of God and that He died for our sins and rose again. It is a sovereign gift of God, which we cannot earn through our good works.

> *For it is by grace that you have been saved through **faith** and not of yourself but it is a gift of God not of works, lest anyone should boast* (Ephesians 2:8).

> *… no one can say that Jesus is Lord except by the Holy Spirit* (1 Corinthians 12:3).

General Faith

Next, there's general faith. This is found in Romans 12:3:

> *For I say that the grace has been given to everyone who is among you not to think more highly of yourself than you ought to but to think soberly. God has in placed in every one of you **a measure of faith**.*

God has deposited in each one of us a certain degree of faith. That means we all have the ability to trust God in our ordinary daily routine. However, if you never exercise that measure of faith, it will never manifest in your life. It's like working out. You couldn't pick up 100 pounds on the first day. But once you start with smaller weights to build up that muscle, 100 pounds is no sweat.

It's the same with your general faith. It starts off small to build up your faith muscle. For instance, you believe that God will help you with your exam and you study certain topics. All those topics come out and you pass. Oh, how thankful you are! Then you are believing God for a new mobile phone, then for a better job. But you have to start somewhere and it will manifest. I remember when I first got saved, all I had the faith for was asking God for a parking space close to the entrance … and somebody would just pull out. I was so thrilled: "Thank You, Jesus. I know You love me, thank You, thank You!"

Fruit of Faithfulness

We studied faithfulness as a fruit of the Holy Spirit in Chapter 5. That's in Galatians 5:22: "… *the fruit of the Spirit is love, joy, peace, longsuffering, kindness, goodness, and faithfulness.*" So in the fruit of faithfulness, the Holy Spirit empowers you to lead a lifestyle of trusting Him no matter what the uncertainties.

GIFT OF FAITH

The gift of faith goes beyond faithfulness, natural trust or expectation. It is a supernatural impartation of belief and confidence that God will act on your behalf in a very radical way. You have that supernatural ability to believe God will come through without any doubt or unbelief or human reasoning. You just know it, you don't have to reason it out, you don't have to figure out how it's going to happen. You just have that surge of faith in God … and then it manifests! When it manifests, that's called a miracle.

Let me give you some examples in the bible about faith in action.

Daniel in the lions' den demonstrates the operation of the gift of faith. When Daniel was cast into the lions' den for praying to his God, God supernaturally closed the mouths of the lions. Daniel was able to spend the whole night in the company of these beasts unharmed. On the other hand, King Darius was so anxious for Daniel, he could not sleep all night. He really didn't want it to happen but his hands were tied. Early the next morning the king rushes to the lions' den. "Hey Daniel, are you still down there?" he calls in a lamenting voice. What a relief to hear Daniel's voice! "Yeah, I'm good!" and Daniel emerges without a scratch (see Daniel 6:1-23). Daniel's faith leads to a miracle.

Someone may say, "That's no miracle! The lions were tame and they'd just been fed." Read on, my friend. When Daniel's accusers were thrown into the same lions' den as punishment, "*the lions overpowered them, and broke all their bones in pieces before they ever came to the bottom of the den*" (Daniel 6:24).

Another gift of faith in action is seen in the Hebrew boys Shadrach, Meshach and Abednego. When they refused to bow down to the golden image in spite of the threat of being thrown into the burning fiery furnace, they calmly replied: "We are not bowing down. Our God will deliver us. Furthermore, know what, O Nebechadnezzar, even if our God doesn't deliver us, we are not going to bow down to your golden image" (see Daniel 3:8-18).

Daniel's three friends were then bound and cast into the flames. The furnace had been heated seven times hotter so much so the heat immediately killed the men who put them in. But Shadrach, Meshach and Abednego were not burned, not even singed. A miracle was taking place! In fact, the king said he saw four men walking in the flames, and the fourth looked like *"the Son of God."* It was Jesus in the fire with them! The three young men emerged from the fire unscathed (see Daniel 3:19-28).

Another gift of faith in action is the prophet Elijah. Because of the famine God told him to drink from the brook and he would be fed by the ravens. God supernaturally sustained him through the ravens who fed him bread and meat in the morning and evening (see 1 Kings 17:2-6).

In my own family, we had our Uncle Bishop Hughue Alexander Wilson who was a preacher. He was born in 1922 in Waxhaw, North Carolina. He was my grandmother's (Leola Wilson Simpson's) baby brother. He relocated to Cleveland and established Holy Temple Church, and was the overseer of the Early Churches of God in Christ. One day one of his members called him to visit a very sick man. When he got there, the man was already dead. However, Uncle Hughue didn't know that the man was already dead. With all his might he prayed for that man and the man came back to life. Under the power of God the dead were raised, the lame walked, minds were restored and hearts mended spiritually and naturally. I believe that generational blessing, hallelujah, is on my life in my bloodline! Uncle Hughue walked in demonstration of all three of the power gifts: he had the FAITH, the people received MIRACLES, and the supernatural Power of God in HEALINGS.

GIFT OF MIRACLES

The gift of faith seems like a passive action. All you have to do is receive it and believe. But you do have to act on it. When you move in the gift of miracles, then it's you acting upon your gift of faith. The miracle is the supernatural power to intervene in the ordinary course of nature and counteract natural and scientific laws. The hand of God steps in to alter our natural circumstances in a way that defies human logic. So when dramatic things happen and there is no reasonable explanation for them, that's the working of miracles.

When Jesus turned the water into wine at the marriage feast of Cana, it was the gift of miracles at work. His mother comes over to Him, "They don't have any wine." He asks what that has to do with Him. She turns to the servants, "Whatever He says to you, do it." So Jesus told the servants to go and fill the water pots with water. They filled the pots with water. They drew the liquid out, and then served the master of the feast. He immediately congratulated the host with, "You have saved the good wine for the last" (see John 2:1-10).

Remember the time Peter walked on water (Matthew 14:22-33)? Peter and the disciples were in the boat buffeted by the wind and the waves. Then, seeing Jesus walking on the water, Peter cried out, "Lord if that's You, tell me to come to You on the water." Jesus told him to come, and Peter started walking on the water. He was walking on the word that Jesus had given him. Did you hear me? He was walking on the Word of God! Hallelujah! We, too, can walk on everything that God puts into our heart through the special revelation God gives us for that moment. It's called the *rhema* word.

Another miracle was Elijah and the widow of Zarephath. In the midst of the famine God tells Elijah to go to this widow and she will provide for him. Elijah finds that this widow is about to prepare the last meal for herself and her son before they die of starvation. Elijah orders her to first make some bread for him with these words: *"For thus says the LORD God of Israel: 'The bin of flour shall not be used up, nor shall the jar of oil run dry, until the day the LORD sends rain on the earth.'"* She did as she was told and the miracle unfolded: there was food in the house as long as the famine lasted (see 1 Kings 17:8-16).

You, too, can experience a miracle when you have a special *rhema* word from God. You've got to act it out by faith. You have to believe that God will work on your behalf. With just the gift of faith, you sit there waiting on God: "Lord, I believe this will happen!" and the manifestation takes place. For a miracle, you have to step out in faith and do something.

GIFTS OF HEALINGS

The last power gifts are the gifts of healings. They refer to healing all manner of sicknesses supernaturally without human aid or medicine. Notice "the gifts of healings" is in the plural, because there are several gifts to heal different kinds of sickness and disease.

Supernatural Power

When God heals you through the exercise of these gifts, it's supernatural. It follows in the path of Jesus *"... how God anointed Jesus of Nazareth with the Holy Spirit and with power, who went about doing good and healing all who were oppressed by the devil, for God was with Him* (Acts 10:38). This scripture reveals two things.

The first is that those who are sick are generally oppressed by the devil. We can already see a clear link between sickness and demonic oppression. Most healing starts in the soul. Note the many times Jesus healed where He rebuked the sickness or cast out the spirit, for instance, Peter's mother-in-law with very high fever (see Luke 4:38-

40), the man whose son had a deaf and dumb spirit (see Mark 9:14-29; Matthew 17:14-16).

The second thing is that Jesus went about healing all who were oppressed. How many did He heal? All. Christ has already provided for our supernatural healing on the cross: "*… who Himself bore our sins in His own body on the tree, that we, having died to sins, might live for righteousness—by whose stripes you were healed*" (1 Peter 2:24). When we are ill, we run to the doctor, when as Christians, we should first seek God to find out the cause and the remedy. Go back to your faith, and see what God wants you to do. If it's to seek medical help, then by all means see the doctor. Let's start with Jesus: seek ye first the Kingdom.

Diversities of Healings Gifts

Gifts of healings are present in the body of Christ and diversities of the same gift are given to different individuals. So one person can have the gift to pray for your headache and it goes away. Another can have the gift to pray for your back and it stops hurting. Somebody else can have the gift to pray for you and diabetes falls off. Other members have a special anointing for cancers, or Alzheimer's, or arthritis, or skin disease or a spinal disorder. So you can operate in different gifts, but God can use anybody at any given time, any way He wants, to help others be healed.

Not only are the healings diverse, God's methods of healing are rarely the same. Naaman the Syrian commander was instructed by Elisha to go wash in the Jordan seven times for his leprosy to be cured. This was a great blow to his ego! But finally he was persuaded to get into the dirtiest of rivers and, on the seventh dip, the leprosy totally left him and his skin was as smooth as a baby (see 2 Kings 5:1-14). On the other hand, the healing of the ten lepers by Jesus was activated when they obeyed His word, "*Go, show yourselves to the priests.*" And so **as they went**, they were cleansed (see Luke 17:11-19).

In the case of Job, the Lord told his three self-righteous friends to offer sacrifices and ask Job to pray for them. When the sacrifices were made and Job prayed for his friends, Job was completely healed and restored of all his possessions (see Job 42:7-10).

When we walk in the gifts of healings, sometimes we are prompted by the Holy Spirit to make a blanket statement and everybody gets healed. Any health problems the people have simply disappear. At other times the word of knowledge is in operation together with the unction to call out certain medical conditions. As people respond, they are healed. In all things God gets all the glory!

Remember, too, that healing is not restricted to the church leaders. Anyone who has the gift can heal because this is one of the signs of the believer:

> "*And these signs will follow **those who believe**: In My name they will cast out demons; they will speak with new tongues; they will take up serpents; and if they drink anything deadly, it will by no means hurt them; they will lay hands on the sick, and they will recover*" (Mark 16:17-18).

One final question: can the faith of the people affect the faith of the minister, the miracles and the healings? Yes, it most certainly can. Two people touched Jesus by their great faith. The woman with the issue of blood literally touched Jesus' at the hem of His garment and His healing virtue flowed out (see Luke 8:43-48). The centurion – a Gentile – had faith to believe that Jesus had only to speak the word from a distance and his servant would be healed. Jesus, amazed that He had not found such faith in all of Israel, spoke the word and the servant was healed that very hour (see Luke 7:1-10).

Notice that Jesus could not do many miracles in His hometown Nazareth because of unbelief, whereas some of Jesus' most outstanding miracles happened in his ministry base Capernaum because the people believed (see Matthew 13:58; Mark 1:32-34).

When our meetings are saturated with the presence of God through our praise, worship and joyful expectation, the healing anointing flows with greater intensity. Give God all the praise! Hallelujah!! Hallelujah!! Hallelujah!!

Chapter 10

THE GIFTS OF THE SPIRIT
-THE GIFTS THAT SAY SOMETHING:
THE INSPIRATIONAL GIFTS-

The three inspirational gifts are gifts of utterance or gifts that say something. They are Tongues, Interpretation of Tongues and Prophecy. These gifts are given for the purpose of edification. "To edify" comes from the Greek *oikodome* (from *oikos*, "a home," and *demo*, "to build"), which means "the act of building." What are we building up? Our own spirit and the spirits of people.

TONGUES

The gifts of speaking in tongues and the interpretation of tongues are perhaps the most controversial of all the gifts. There are many objections to them. These objections come especially from traditional churches as well as believers who have strong views about the relevance of such gifts in this day and age.

Let's first look at some of the objections to speaking in tongues and see how we can address them.

Objection 1: No longer relevant

Many people believe tongues were confined to the days of the early church when great signs and wonders were necessary to convince the people of the new move of God. When the Holy Spirit fell upon the disciples on the day of Pentecost and they started speaking in other tongues, on that day itself over 3,000 souls were drawn to Christ (see Acts 2:1-40).

Yes, there is no doubt that signs and wonders were necessary in the early church to break through the stronghold of tradition. Well, if that was true of the early church, what more in these end times when our society is flooded by so many false doctrines and secularism?

Again, if all the gifts are necessary for all times, why do people have difficulty accepting the gift of tongues?

Whatever our human reasoning tells us, we cannot argue against Jesus' specific command that tongues are to be used as one the signs manifested by the believer:

> *And these signs will follow those who believe: In My name they will cast out demons; they will speak with new tongues; they will take up serpents; and if they drink anything deadly, it will by no means hurt them; they will lay hands on the sick, and they will recover"* (Mark 16:17-18).

Most people have no problem believing in casting out demons and healing. Why then do they single out tongues as something that is no longer relevant?

Objection 2: Fear

Perhaps their objection is that they feel uncomfortable speaking aloud in tongues. It looks odd and may cause people to laugh at us.

But that's exactly what Paul says concerning the "*foolish*" and "*weak*" things that God uses to shame the wise and mighty.

> *But God has chosen the foolish things of the world to put to shame the wise, and God has chosen the weak*

> *things of the world to put to shame the things which are mighty ...* (1 Corinthians 1:27).

Many of us like to look cool on the outside – like everybody else. Very often we find safety in conformity, not being the odd one out. But God is looking for people who dare to face ridicule and never be ashamed of Him. So speaking in tongues is a real test of our faith. It is teaching us to overcome the fear of man and our own doubts especially when we don't know what we are praying.

> *For if I pray in a tongue, my spirit prays, but my understanding is unfruitful...* (1 Corinthians 14:14)

Another kind of fear is wondering what kind of spirit we are receiving when we receive the gift of tongues. Is it of God or of an evil spirit?

Jesus gives us the answer.

> *"If a son asks for bread from any father among you, will he give him a stone? Or if he asks for a fish, will he give him a serpent instead of a fish? Or if he asks for an egg, will he offer him a scorpion? If you then, being evil, know how to give good gifts to your children, how much more will your heavenly Father give the Holy Spirit to those who ask Him!"* (Luke 11:11-13)

It's interesting that Jesus chose those two images – serpents and scorpions. Remember Luke 10:19 when He mentioned giving us authority over serpents and scorpions? They represent demonic spirits. Do you think the Father would give His beloved child an evil spirit when you come to Him in faith trusting Him for good gifts? Surely He will give you the Holy Spirit, nothing less!

Objection 3: Genuine and fake tongues

The greatest amount of controversy relating to tongues is the endless debate about genuine tongues and fake tongues.

The proponents of "genuine tongues" point to the Day of Pentecost when the Holy Spirit fell on all the disciples and they began speaking in tongues. The tongues they spoke were in a language unknown to them but were understood by the many Jews visiting Jerusalem from other parts of Asia. So here we have tongues which are unknown to the speakers but known to the wider audience. The audience knew that these men coming from Galilee had no way of knowing their languages but were, nevertheless, praising God in a way that was understood by foreigners. This phenomenon, followed by the learned address by Peter the uneducated fisherman, was a sign and wonder that something supernatural was happening right there. It had a huge impact on the crowd. No wonder 3,000 came to the Lord that very day!

The same phenomenon exists even today. We have no problem accepting the fact that we may supernaturally speak in a language known to an audience in a country we are visiting. For instance, you may be traveling to Kenya and speak in a tongue unknown to yourself but known to a Swahili speaking audience!

Does this mean that all tongues must be in a language known to some people group? The argument goes that those whose tongues have no reference to any known language are just speaking in babble, or fake tongues!

But look at what the word of God says: *"Though I speak with the tongues of men and of angels ..."* (1 Corinthians 13:1). This means that in addition to the "tongues of men" i.e. known languages, there is such a thing as "tongues of angels." This is a heavenly language, not known to man. Who understands this heavenly language? I'm glad you asked. The answer is found in 1 Corinthians 14:3: *"For he who speaks in a tongue does not speak to men but to God, for no one understands him; however, in the spirit **he speaks mysteries**"*(emphasis added).

So when you speak in tongues, you may be communicating with someone in the audience in their native language. This can happen.

But, for the most part, you are pouring your heart out to God in a private language given by the Holy Spirit that only He understands.

We have a choice to make. To be wise and follow the thinking of the world? Or to be foolish and honor God? Dear reader, do not allow anyone to talk you out of using this special heavenly language given by the Holy Spirit. You are walking by faith and not by sight as you open yourself to being led by the Holy Spirit on an adventure like nothing you've experienced before.

Benefits of Tongues

Tongues are generally the first sign we are filled with the Holy Spirit. We see this throughout the Book of Acts of all who were baptized in the Holy Spirit. When people received Jesus as their Savior, they almost immediately received the baptism of the Holy Spirit with the evidence of speaking in tongues. It follows that every one of us who has been baptized in the Holy Spirit should be speaking in tongues. If you are not, then examine yourself and ask whether it is your own prejudices that are blocking the flow of the Holy Spirit.

Once you know the benefits of speaking in tongues, you will want this gift at all costs.

- **Never lost for words**

  Suddenly our prayer life becomes rich and exciting. We find we have a variety of tongues for different occasions: praise tongues, warfare tongues, intercessory tongues with groaning that cannot be expressed (see Romans 8:26).

- **Build ourselves up in our faith** (see Jude 20).

  Anyone who is continually in the presence of God, speaking mysteries to Him, cannot fail but be built up in their faith.

- **Facilitate the release of other gifts**

  As you speak in tongues, your faith is rising. This makes you more sensitive to hearing from God – in a vision, a prompting, a scripture. When your faith is built, you are more able to move in any of the other gifts: word of knowledge, word of wisdom, prophecy, healings or greater faith to believe in miracles.

- **Bring us refreshing and rest** (see Isaiah 28:2).

    In the presence of God there is fullness of joy. There is peace. As you cast your cares upon Him, He will refresh you.

- **Cause rivers of living water to flow** (see John 7:37-39).

    The rivers of living water are the filling of the Holy Spirit. When you have the Holy Spirit in full to overflowing, you are releasing life and abundance to all those around you.

I remember vividly the first time I received the gift of tongues I had been a member of a Christian fellowship center for many years. They would have altar calls for people to come up and receive the gift of tongues, but for some reason, I never went up to the front. I never went up to be prayed for to receive the gift of the heavenly language. But I always desired the gift.

One day I had a conversation with my spiritual mother who is also my cousin, Pastor Pamela Westbrook of Agape Christian Canter in Virginia, and we talked about me not speaking in tongues. I met her at the church office and she prayed for me. First, she taught me a few scriptures from the Book of Acts about the Day of Pentecost and then she prayed with me and said, "OK, my daughter, open your mouth and speak." So I opened my mouth and I heard these strange words coming out, and stopped. She said "OK ... you have the gift of tongues ... I'll see you later."

I was like, "Really! I have the gift of tongues??? That's it???"

She said, "Yeah, you got it; didn't you hear yourself??"

"YESSSS!!! I heard myself. But that was so simple! That's it? I got it? I got the gift of tongues?"

"Yes, my daughter!"

As soon as I got in the car I began to speak in tongues and they got louder. It also seemed like the tongues were changing and I spoke in tongues all the way to my destination.

That night before I went to bed I started praying in tongues. Do you know, I did not stop until 5 am the next morning. I was thinking I was going to be tired as I had to be at the salon & spa to open it at 8 am. BUT to my surprise I had so much energy and joy ... the clients kept telling me I was glowing!

INTERPRETATION OF TONGUES

Many believers have been led to believe that all tongues must be interpreted. In other words, you must know the meaning of what you are saying. If the meaning is not given, either by the tongues-speaker or by another, then the tongues are not valid. If this is true, then 90% of the tongues we speak are fake, and this adds yet another argument for those who oppose tongues.

But let us look more closely at the scriptures that may have led to some misunderstanding.

> *Pursue love, and desire spiritual gifts, but especially that you may prophesy. For he who speaks in a tongue does not speak to men but to God, for no one understands him; however, in the spirit he speaks mysteries. But he who prophesies speaks edification and exhortation and comfort to men. He who speaks in a tongue edifies himself, but he who prophesies edifies the church. I wish you all spoke with tongues, but even more that you prophesied; for he who prophesies is greater than he who speaks with tongues, unless indeed he interprets, that the church may receive edification* (1 Corinthians 14:1-5).

Verse 5 is key: "*I wish you all spoke with tongues, but even more that you prophesied; for he who prophesies is greater than he who* *speaks with tongues, **unless indeed he interprets, that the church may receive edification**.*" When Paul says "*for he who prophesies is greater than he who speaks with tongues, **unless indeed he interprets** ...*" it seems that he is referring to two different kinds of tongues: "*speaks with tongues*" i.e. normal tongues without interpretation and tongues with interpretation. Normal tongues are tongues you and I speak in the privacy of our home or some quiet place. We may even speak them together with other believers in church; but no one is dominating. They are a personal communication between us and God. We are speaking mysteries that we don't normally understand but they communicate something to God.

On the other hand, tongues with interpretation come with prophecy. They are spoken at a gathering of believers in a church meeting or fellowship. When a speaker raises his voice in the middle of the service to break forth in tongues, this is a sign that God has an important message for the whole church. What must at once follow is the interpretation in the language of the audience. This should be given by the speaker himself or any other believer in the congregation. If there is no interpretation, then the one who spoke should be silent and not continue in tongues.

> *If anyone speaks in a tongue, let there be two or at the most three, each in turn, and let one interpret. But if there is no interpreter, let him keep silent in church, and let him speak to himself and to God* (1 Corinthians 14:27-28).

For if there is no interpretation, Paul quite rightly wonders how the message can be received without understanding?

> *But now, brethren, if I come to you speaking with tongues, what shall I profit you unless I speak to you either by revelation, by knowledge, by prophesying, or by teaching? ... So likewise you, unless you utter by the tongue words easy to understand, how will it be*

> *known what is spoken? For you will be speaking into the air ... Therefore let him who speaks in a tongue pray that he may interpret* (1 Corinthians 14:6,9,13).

What tongues is Paul referring to? Tongues with interpretation, of course. In the next verse, Paul concludes that we should use both kinds of tongues – tongues without interpretation and tongues with interpretation – but in the right settings. He says he uses tongues more than anybody else; yet he rarely uses tongues in the church. We should take our cue from him and be very cautious about initiating tongues that require interpretation, unless we have a strong prompting from the Lord.

> *What is the conclusion then? I will pray with the spirit, and I will also pray with the understanding. I will sing with the spirit, and I will also sing with the understanding ... I thank my God I speak with tongues more than you all; yet **in the church** I would rather speak five words with my understanding, that I may teach others also, than ten thousand words in a tongue* (1 Corinthians 14:15-16;18-19).

Since interpretation of tongues and prophecy are closely related, we will continue this discussion when we look at the gift of prophecy shortly.

Translation vs. Interpretation

But for now, I would like to address another misconception about interpreting tongues. Interpretation of tongues is not a direct TRANSLATION; it is an INTERPRETATION. Let me illustrate. Sister Julie stands up and delivers a short message in tongues to the church. It takes only one minute. Then Sister Sandra stands up and gives an interpretation in English (or whatever the language of the house may be). She uses many words and gestures, and it takes at least five minutes. Question: Was Sister Sandra genuine? Was that interpretation accurate?

The answer to both questions is "Yes," assuming that both speakers were led by the Holy Spirit. You see, interpretation of tongues is not a word-for-word or verbatim translation of the tongues being released. Rather, it is the supernatural ability to interpret in a known language the most important point of the message. The person with the gift of interpreting tongues can discern what God is putting across through the tongues-speaker. They would then communicate the meaning of the message to everyone else, so all could understand.

"But why doesn't the Holy Spirit just convey the message in a known language?" you ask. Good question. Could the answer be found in 1 Corinthians 14 verse 22? *"Therefore tongues are for a sign, not to those who believe but to **unbelievers**; but prophesying is not for unbelievers but for those who believe."* Tongues are a sign to the unbeliever. I've always wondered about that. Different people have different explanations for this. But I have come to believe this. God wishes to demonstrate to the unbeliever visiting the church that the Spirit of God is moving in this place and both tongues-speaker and interpreter are His mouthpiece. Who knows, the message may be the answer to the questions the unbeliever came asking. God is speaking to unbelievers in a way that will open their eyes to the supernatural.

In my experience when tongues need to be translated or interpreted, first an atmosphere has been set. I have experienced in various church services that several times, in the midst of praising God and praying in our heavenly led language, all of a sudden somebody's tongues will get really loud as if they have a megaphone in front of their mouth. And then all the other tongues would just kind of slow down, get quiet and cease. And then that person will continue speaking in their heavenly language till they are done. There would normally be a little silence, after which either the tongues speaker or someone who by the Spirit has the interpretation of those tongues would come forth with a message, saying, "Thus says the Lord …" and deliver a corporate message. It will be a message to uplift the body of Christ.

Let me stress again that speaking in tongues and interpreting tongues are both gifts given to individuals as the Holy Spirit decides, as Paul says in 1 Corinthians 12:11. So we cannot claim any credit for that ability, or believe we are more spiritual than others, any more than someone gifted with supernatural healing can claim credit for it.

I hope that brings clarity to the interpretation of tongues. It is real and is taking place and should not be suppressed. God does have a message for His people TODAY!!

PROPHECY

Edification, Exhortation and Comfort

Of all the gifts of the Holy Spirit, Paul urges us to desire the gift of prophecy. What is his reason for saying this? Let's look at the key verses about prophecy in 1 Corinthians 14.

> *Pursue love, and desire spiritual gifts, but especially that you may prophesy. For he who speaks in a tongue does not speak to men but to God, for no one understands him; however, in the spirit he speaks mysteries. But he who prophesies speaks edification and exhortation and comfort to men. He who speaks in a tongue edifies himself, but he who prophesies edifies the church. I wish you all spoke with tongues, but even more that you prophesied; for he who prophesies is greater than he who speaks with tongues, unless indeed he interprets, that the church may receive edification. Even so you, since you are zealous for spiritual gifts, let it be for the edification of the church that you seek to excel* (1 Corinthians 14:1-5; 12).

The reason that prophecy is higher than any other gift is because it **edifies** or builds up the body of Christ. Therefore it is superior to [personal] tongues which edify just the individual. Paul also elevates the interpretation of tongues to the level of prophecy because it, too, seeks to edify the whole body.

Along with edification, prophecy also seeks to exhort and comfort.

To exhort is to encourage or urge someone to go higher. For example, a speaker could exhort the church to holiness, consecration and separation from the world at a time when members are facing challenges. When the devil discourages us, it's the prophetic word that will lift us up.

And, closely linked with exhortation is **comfort**. Comfort is a state of freedom from pain or constraint or the easing of a person's feelings of grief or distress. A prophetic word that brings hope to people who are in distress will also comfort them by the assurance that God is close to them.

Both exhortation and comfort release supernatural strength to the hearers. They may need that prophetic word to hold on to their core values in the midst of pressures from society.

Let me illustrate. In today's liberal society the whole LGBTQ is such a BIG DEAL and we are told we have to love everybody… otherwise we are committing a hate crime. I love the person and hate the sin (because God hates SIN).

Homosexual desire is not what God originally intend or ever intended. All of our desires have been distorted by sin. But Paul does describe both lesbian and male homosexual behaviour as "unnatural" in Romans 1:24-25. Paul says that homosexual behaviour contradicts the nature God gave us, as revealed in creation and reiterated throughout Scripture.

However, proponents of the gay agenda argue that the concept of 'natural" is in relation to what individuals **feel is natural** for themselves. So what is in view is heterosexual people engaging in homosexual activity and thereby going against their "natural" orientation. But God's word is very clear and specific and cannot be twisted by clever argument. Homosexuality is fundamentally wrong.

But don't belabor things. We also need to understand that homosexuals have wrestled long and hard with the decision to come out of the closet and openly declare their orientation. I am sure they braced themselves for judgment and rejection. That's why it's all the more important that we let them know they are valued and loved as much as ever. It's especially important that whatever statements you make be couched in love. The important message remains: "I love you and accept you" — that will never change.

At the same time, as believers, we should not be silenced about stating our concerns about the morality, health risks and potential dangers involved with the gay lifestyle. We will continue to speak out against all forms of sexual behavior which challenge God's laws: promiscuity, adultery, homosexual activity, lesbianism, and pedophilia.

Once the law made same sex marriages legal in Ohio, we had to amend our church's by-laws to include language that made our stance clear about the role of leaders in our church and our non acceptance of ALL forms of sexual immorality.

False Prophets

It is important that we make a distinction between prophesying and fortune-telling or forecasting future events. Prophecy is not fortune-telling; it is, more correctly, forth-telling. In other words, the prophet is speaking out the mind of Christ, delivering a timely word to encourage and build up the people. If we view prophecy in this light, we will not come with the false expectation of wanting to know the future but come to receive the Lord's encouragement.

Much of bible prophecy since the days of the Old Testament prophets such as Isaiah and Jeremiah has already been fulfilled in the life of Jesus. What remains are the prophecies in the book of Revelation, Daniel, Isaiah, Ezekiel, Joel and others that will be fulfilled at the end of the age. So for the most part, the prophetic word given by a modern prophet is not some new revelation. Rather, it is an affirmation, application or interpretation of something that has already been prophesied.

We would all agree that this is a time of great instability and uncertainty across the nations. People are seeking answers to the things that are troubling them and will seek out people who can provide them with answers. And many church leaders may desire to accommodate them. We must take heed, lest we be deceived by false teaching. Paul warns us of a time when people will want come to the prophet with itching ears, not wanting to know sound doctrine but to justify their position or lifestyle:

> *For the time will come when they will not endure sound doctrine, but according to their own desires, because they have itching ears, they will heap up for themselves teachers; and they will turn their ears away from the truth, and be turned aside to fables* (2 Timothy 4:3-4).

I wonder why there are so many of us with itching ears? Could it be that we have an attention deficit because there is so much information flying around in this digital age? Nowhere is the need to be grounded in the word more critical as in these last days, for this is a time of great apostasy. We need to be sober and heed Jesus' warnings about many false prophets appearing in these last days:

> *Then many false prophets will rise up and deceive many. And because lawlessness will abound, the love of many will grow cold. But he who endures to the end shall be saved ... For false christs and false prophets will rise and show great signs and wonders to deceive, if possible, even the elect. See, I have told you beforehand* (Matthew 24:11-13; 24-25).

This is indeed a time of great lawlessness for the United States as well as the rest of the world. The moral values we have held as a

Christian nation are being challenged by a new set of norms. These norms are based on a belief system called humanism which places its value on the human perspective of life and society, not on God's. It presents man as a rational evolved being and therefore capable of saying that God's laws as revealed in the bible are obsolete.

In the above scripture, Jesus then makes a very sobering claim. He says that many false christs and false prophets will rise and deceive us through great signs and wonders. Do you see this happening in the church already? Many of our church meetings are full of hype. But is it of God? Not all those signs and wonders are released by the power of the Holy Spirit. However, many will be deceived, even the elect. And, if the elect (the specially-chosen ones) could be deceived, then we know Jesus is speaking about the church. Satan uses the church setting through unsanctified ministers to show his signs and wonders. How do we know which is which?

My friends, let us never forget there are TWO INVISIBLE SPIRITUAL KINGDOMS – the kingdom of God and the kingdom of satan. The kingdom of God is automatically at war with the kingdom of satan … you choose your side. When you got saved, you showed YOU ARE ON THE LORD'S SIDE and you are no longer governed by the kingdom of satan.

However, as our society evolves, many of us are subject to a slow conditioning process. We are being steeped in a world with changing values where black becomes white and white becomes black. Most of our television shows now have homosexual characters. Five years ago all this blurring of genders, sexual fluidity and asexual identity was unheard of – it is heart breaking that our society is being deceived on a grand scale.

But often we say nothing for the sake of showing tolerance or for fear of being branded —-haters! Slowly by slowly we are being compromised. We mouth things that are politically correct to gain acceptance.

So the church is in danger of losing our voice as the light and the salt. But many out there need the comfort of religion. If the church should no longer be the answer, there are dozens of other ways of seeking the truth in the eyes of society. The dominant one is new spirituality or new age thinking based on human consciousness. It even accepts Christ by presenting its own version of the universal Christ, fashioned in its own image. In this new spirituality, the word "sin" is not mentioned because man is continuing to evolve towards perfection. If there is no sin, it follows there is no need for Jesus to die for sin. We don't need a Savior. There is no judgment. There is no hell. The Christ we have fashioned simply tells us to carry on in our permissive lifestyle.

Didn't Jesus warn us of the coming of another Christ, not the Jewish Messiah who died for sin?

> *"Then if anyone says to you, 'Look, here is the Christ!' or 'There!' do not believe it. "Therefore if they say to you, 'Look, He is in the desert!' do not go out; or 'Look, He is in the inner rooms!' do not believe it. For as the lightning comes from the east and flashes to the west, so also will the coming of the Son of Man be"* (Matthew 24:23-27).

But Christ will come at the appointed time in all His glory. The false christ – the antichrist –will be exposed.

My challenge to you is: Are you going to believe in the word of God or in the profusion of prophetic words running through YouTube or the social media any day? Who do we believe? Like the Bereans who checked every teaching, we need to test the prophetic word being spoken even within the church against the scriptures. For no prophetic word must be based on any individual interpretation. It must line up with the word.

> *...no prophecy of Scripture is of any private interpretation, for prophecy never came by the will of*

man, but holy men of God spoke as they were moved by the Holy Spirit (2 Peter 1:20-21).

Secondly, we need to test the spirits to know what kind of spirit is behind the message:

"Beloved, do not believe every spirit, but test the spirits, whether they are of God; because many false prophets have gone out into the world" (1 John 4:1).

Thirdly, we need to test the character of the prophet. In other words, test the fruit of the Spirit in their life. Jesus' warnings for this age are so timely:

"Beware of false prophets, who come to you in sheep's clothing, but inwardly they are ravenous wolves. You will know them by their fruits. Do men gather grapes from thorn bushes or figs from thistles? Even so, every good tree bears good fruit, but a bad tree bears bad fruit. A good tree cannot bear bad fruit, nor can a bad tree bear good fruit. Every tree that does not bear good fruit is cut down and thrown into the fire. Therefore by their fruits you will know them" (Matthew 7:15-20).

I remember my husband Apostle Greg and me once going to a service where a well-known young prophet was the guest speaker. Now this young man was on point ... he preached, he taught the word of God, he was entertaining and revelatory all in the same service. I think we were there for five hours and not one person left the service. The next day we got word that the young prophet had young women at his hotel room after service – and they were not praying! I felt so grieved. We have to look beyond the anointing to the CHARACTER and the FRUIT!!!

CONCLUSION

In light of our discussion, what have we learned about prophecy? Prophecy is a supernatural utterance not conceived by human thought or reasoning. It can be delivered in a known language or in public tongues. In the case of tongues, there must be interpretation of the tongues in a language known to the house. The three functions of edifying, exhorting and comforting are demonstrations of God pouring out His love, compassion and hope on His people. Let us always remember that *"the testimony of Jesus is the spirit of prophecy"* (Revelation 19:10). So let us take care that all prophecy reflects the heart of Jesus and glorifies God, not the messenger.

CHAPTER 11

"BLOW THE TRUMPET IN ZION"

This has been an exciting journey as we've begun to discover more about the Holy Spirit and invite Him into our lives. We know that He is God, the 3rd person of the Triune God and that He is integrally related to God the Father and God the Son. The Holy Spirit is a Person, not a force or energy, and He has a distinct personality that expresses itself in joy, in peace, and the sparkle of new wine. He also brings chastisement and can be grieved by our hardened hearts. Above all, He is the One that Jesus has given to be our Counselor, Teacher and Friend as we go through all of life's challenges.

When we receive the Holy Spirit, we become open to supernatural Gifts whenever He releases them. These gifts are intended to empower us to witness Jesus to the world and minister to the lost with healings, signs and wonders. And, as we allow our spirit, soul and senses to be remolded by Him, we will see changes in our character and begin to display His Fruit, reflecting Christ. It is the fruit that give us the strength of character to contain the anointing.

Are you happy to be alive and have the Holy Spirit walking with you? Do you want more of Him so that He can continue to do His marvelous work of changing you and making you a ready vessel for the Lord?

Darkness over the Earth

My brother, my sister, you and I are living in momentous times! If there is one word that can be used to epitomize the times we are living in – it's CHANGE. Not always for good though. There is an acceleration of evil coming into the world. At the same time there is an acceleration of love and power penetrating the darkness. If we remain passive we will be swept away in the evil tide. But if we choose to declare our stand for God and take up our weapons, we will arise and shine for His glory.

I want to spend this time talking about the end times and the alarming changes we are seeing in our society with particular emphasis to the United States. The Bible says that there is nothing new under the sun, so what is happening now, what we are required to do and what is the outcome have already been predicted in the Bible.

The Joel 2 Prophecy

When Peter addressed the multitude on the Day of Pentecost, the scripture he quoted was from Joel Chapter 2:

> *"And it shall come to pass in the last days, says God,*
> *That I will pour out of My Spirit on all flesh;*
> *Your sons and your daughters shall prophesy,*
> *Your young men shall see visions,*
> *Your old men shall dream dreams.*
> *And on My menservants and on My maidservants*
> *I will pour out My Spirit in those days;*
> *And they shall prophesy.*
>
> *"I will show wonders in heaven above*
> *And signs in the earth beneath:*
> *Blood and fire and vapor of smoke.*
> *The sun shall be turned into darkness,*
> *And the moon into blood,*
> *Before the coming of the great and awesome day of the* Lord.
> *And it shall come to pass*
> *That whoever calls on the name of the* Lord
> *Shall be saved"* (Acts 2:17-21).

It is significant that Peter should use this scripture because it highlighted a mighty move of the Holy Spirit following Pentecost. But it is also interesting that Peter adds another verse in the Joel prophecy: the fearful signs in the heavens that will follow (see Acts 2:19-21). None of those cosmic signs happened in the days of the apostles and yet Peter chooses to include this part of the prophecy. We can only conclude that the Holy Spirit was leading both Joel and Peter to predict to future generations the days to come after the tribulation when cosmic signs will shake the heavens before that *"great and awesome day of the* L*ORD*.*"*

Such a day was also prophesied by Jesus when He was preaching about the tribulation.

> *"Immediately after the tribulation of those days the sun will be darkened, and the moon will not give its light; the stars will fall from heaven, and the powers of the heavens will be shaken. Then the sign of the Son of Man will appear in heaven, and then all the tribes of the earth will mourn, and they will see the Son of Man coming on the clouds of heaven with power and great glory"* (Matthew 24:29-30).

Dear reader, we are the generation living in these final days before the tribulation and the second coming of Jesus. Yes, there will be a mighty outpouring of the Holy Spirit as in the days of Pentecost. This will be followed by the tribulation period culminating in signs in the heavens. But before the final outpouring, like the locust army, there will be judgment. Since there is such a strong parallel between Joel and the times in which we live, it is crucial that we understand the entire scenario to be prepared for change and know what to do.

First, let's get a clearer picture of the actual setting in which the prophet Joel was addressing his audience.

In Joel Chapter 1 and part of Chapter 2, Joel describes a locust invasion in the land of Israel. It is so devastating that the harvest is destroyed and with that the livestock and the entire economy. Throughout the history of Israel, God has dealt with His people's disobedience and apostasy by allowing all kinds of evil to afflict them, from enemy invasion, famine, pestilence, to plagues. Locust attacks were not uncommon but this time it appears as if they are directed by God Himself:

> *The Lord gives voice before **His army**,*
> *For His camp is very great;*
> *For strong is the One who executes His word* (Joel 2:11, emphasis added).

The locusts are His army. They come in highly disciplined waves of attack as if they were orchestrated by an invisible hand:

> *They run like mighty men,*
> *They climb the wall like men of war;*
> *Every one marches in formation,*
> *And they do not break ranks.*
> *They do not push one another;*
> *Every one marches in his own column* (Joel 2:7-8).

What do the locusts represent in our society? In this postmodern era, evil of every form has been creeping into our society: corruption, perversions, violence. We have showed concern but tolerated them to a degree as the people's right to choose. At the same time, there has been increasing pressure on those with godly values to keep silent for fear of being labeled haters of X, Y or Z. So we have maintained "political correctness."

But suddenly as I write, I am witnessing the tide of evil rising to unprecedented levels in American society, and western society as a whole. We tolerated gay lifestyles, then it pushed the boundary to gay marriages, then it entered the church, so we have church-sanctioned gay marriages and even gay pastors! Now the threat to our value system has gone up many notches with the concept of gender fluidity so that our children will be raised in a society with blurred gender identity. Again, the acceptance of early abortions has opened the way to full term abortions – even those advocating "post birth abortions" (let's call it like it is: infanticide!). And pedophilia and child sex trafficking have become a highly organized global movement.

I ask myself whether all these things just sprang up from the ground independently. Or are they part of a concerted attack on fundamental values that we cherish in our society: the distinction between male and female, the definition of marriage, the protection of the young and most vulnerable members of our society. Is this not upping the ante to directly challenge the God of the Bible and values He instituted? What are some of these values?

On gender differentiation:

He created them male and female, and blessed them and called them Mankind in the day they were created (Genesis 5:2).

On marriage:

Therefore a man shall leave his father and mother and be joined to his wife, and they shall become one flesh (Genesis 2:24).

On homosexuality:

For this reason God gave them up to vile passions. For even their women exchanged the natural use for what is against nature. Likewise also the men, leaving the natural use of the woman, burned in their lust for one another, men with men committing what is shameful, and receiving in themselves the penalty of their error which was due (Romans 1:26-27).

On corrupting the young:

"But whoever causes one of these little ones who believe in Me to sin, it would be better for him if a

millstone were hung around his neck, and he were drowned in the depth of the sea" (Matthew 18:6).

On child sacrifice (read abortions) and profaning the name of the LORD:

*"And thou shalt not let any of thy seed pass through the fire to Molech, neither shalt thou profane the name of thy God: I am the L*ORD*"* (Leviticus 18:21 KJV).

Recently, there have been public voices urging us to sever our ties with Israel who has been our strongest ally since its formation in 1948. What does the word of the Lord say to that?

For the Lord of Armies says this: "In pursuit of his glory, he sent me against the nations plundering you, for whoever touches you touches the pupil of my eye" (Zechariah 2:8 CSB).

The locust invasion in our society represents a well-orchestrated tsunami of evil by the enemy. It threatens to bring down our core values of belief in God, morality, decency, justice and respect for life as we know it.

Nowadays people are always speaking about their truth, My truth, your truth, her truth, his truth. As 21st century Christians, we either avoid speaking truth in fear of offending someone, or we speak the truth so harshly that we don't display love at all, but rather a cold, hard somewhat disrespectful attitude. Ephesians 4:15 says as believers we should be "speaking the truth in love." The primary way we reveal our love for God is by loving others. So speak with love.

In the same chapter, Paul had the difficult task of pointing out to these new believers that they needed to steer clear of sexual impurity. Also, some of them had started living in idleness and depending on others for handouts. They were not being responsible and Paul has to reprove them for this behavior.

Absolute truth is something that is true at all times and in all places. It is something that is always true no matter what the circumstances. It is a fact that cannot be changed. The Bible draws the bridge between the head and heart. The Scriptures which consists of 66 books, with over 40 authors written over a span I don't know of how many years – that's My TRUTH.

The question I now ask is have we experienced any of God's judgments? I do not want to be dogmatic on this issue but have we not seen mounting violence, hate crimes as well as out of control fires, tornadoes and other natural disasters? Have we not had our own personal dealings from God?

Yes, as a loving Father, God chastens those He loves:

> *If you endure chastening, God deals with you as with sons; for what son is there whom a father does not chasten? But if you are without chastening, of which all have become partakers, then you are illegitimate and not sons. Furthermore, we have had human fathers who corrected us, and we paid them respect. Shall we not much more readily be in subjection to the Father of spirits and live? For they indeed for a few days chastened us as seemed best to them, but He for our profit, that we may be partakers of His holiness. Now no chastening seems to be joyful for the present, but painful; nevertheless, afterward it yields the peaceable fruit of righteousness to those who have been trained by it* (Hebrews 12:7-11).

Call to Repentance

God is now calling us to repentance both for our own sins and the sins of our nation:

> *"Now, therefore," says the* LORD,
> *"Turn to Me with all your heart,*

With fasting, with weeping, and with mourning."
So rend your heart, and not your garments;
Return to the LORD *your God,*
For He is gracious and merciful,
Slow to anger, and of great kindness;
And He relents from doing harm ... (Joel 2:12-13).

How do we repent?

Blow the Trumpet in Zion

Blow the trumpet in Zion,
Consecrate a fast,
Call a sacred assembly;
Gather the people,
Sanctify the congregation,
Assemble the elders,
Gather the children and nursing babes;
Let the bridegroom go out from his chamber,
And the bride from her dressing room.
Let the priests, who minister to the LORD,
Weep between the porch and the altar;
Let them say, "Spare Your people, O LORD,
And do not give Your heritage to reproach,
That the nations should rule over them.
Why should they say among the peoples,
'Where is their God?'"(Joel 2:15-17)

In Israel the *shofar* or the silver trumpet was used as an alert signal mainly to warn the people of danger and to summon them to assembly. In our context both signals apply:

- The call to prayer
- The call to use our voice as a trumpet

The Call to Prayer

This urgent call applies to all sectors of our believing community from elders to babies. The call is so pressing that God is saying, "I want you to put aside whatever you are doing, whatever you are planning – even if it's a wedding – to come together. I want you to sanctify yourselves, that is, to separate yourself from your normal routine functions, to come together at this sacred assembly."

The call is especially heavy on the church leaders to lead by example in standing in the gap for the nation:

> *Let the priests, who minister to the LORD,*
> *Weep between the porch and the altar;*
> *Let them say, "Spare Your people, O LORD,*
> *And do not give Your heritage to reproach ..."* (verse 17)

But every believer is called for intercession as well. For the word of the Lord says

> *"If My people who are called by My name will humble themselves, and pray and seek My face, and turn from their wicked ways, then I will hear from heaven, and will forgive their sin and heal their land"* (2 Chronicles 7:14).

It is the redeemed of the Lord who are asked to pray for the unredeemed. We need to humble ourselves and bring to the Lord even the perpetrators of evil so that they will be convicted and have a heart change. Our real enemy is not flesh and blood but principalities and powers and the whole host of the demonic realm (See Ephesians 6:12).

There is a place for personal intercession but this is a call for corporate intercession – within your prayer group, or church or prayer ministry or networks. We can meet in church or in our homes, or pray online, as long as we are of one heart, one mind. There is power in agreement because the Lord is standing in the midst of us (see Matthew 18:19-20). The effective fervent prayers of the righteous will avail much (see James 5:16).

You may decide to prayer walk or prayer drive around certain parts of your city that are oppressed. Speak life into dead situations even in the darkest of places.

> *But if the Spirit of Him who raised Jesus from the dead dwells in you, He who raised Christ from the dead will also give life to your mortal bodies through His Spirit who dwells in you* (Romans 8:11).

Make declarations about our nation being righteous. Declare a highway of holiness across America under God's mighty hand. Call the prisoners out from prison doors. Proclaim revival across this nation.

> Praise is one of the greatest warfare weapons, so praise God with declarations.
>
> By His stripes, we are healed!
>
> By His nail-pierced hands, we're free!
>
> By His blood, we're washed clean!
>
> Now we have the victory!
>
> The power of sin is broken!
>
> Jesus overcame it all!
>
> He has won our freedom!
>
> Jesus has won it all!
>
> Hallelujah, You have won the victory!
>
> Hallelujah, You have won it all for me!
>
> Death could not hold You down; You are the risen King!
>
> Seated in majesty, You are the risen King!

Jesus has defeated the power of sin and death, and He offers the benefits of that victory to all who accept the invitation to be part of His family. There's nothing we can do to win what He offers us. That's the point of grace: God has done all the work – all the "winning", if you like – and He offers us the fruit of His victory on a plate. Thank you Jesus!

It would also be good to set aside certain times to fast and pray. If you have never fasted before, now is the time to learn about the different ways of fasting. If you are a church leader, this is the time to declare a fast that will call down God's mercy and cleanse this land (see Isaiah 58:3-10).

Use Our Voice as a Trumpet

We should put feet to our prayer by making our voice heard publicly. Write books, write blogs, use the social media to reach out, campaign for social justice, engage in friendly conversations with people over issues. The abortion debate is a good opportunity to share the good news. But remember to move in a spirit of gentleness and at all times remember to show love.

As the Holy Spirit leads you, be a witness for Christ and share your testimony. Love is the greatest commandment and we as the body of Christ must operate in the love of Christ. Writing this book has been a blessing to me and I pray it is a blessing to you, too, as you allow the Holy Spirit dwelling on the inside of you to lead and guide you in all truth.

We must walk with Christ, turning our back on the world's way of doing things. I pray that your spiritual eyes are open to the traps of the enemy Please know and understand the devil is a liar and he want to deceive you into believing things that are not the truth…the Holy Spirit will expose that deception and reveal the truth of God.

I know the word of God will transform your life.

The Coming Move

> *And it shall come to pass in the last days, says God,*
> *That I will pour out of My Spirit on all flesh;*
> *Your sons and your daughters shall prophesy,*
> *Your young men shall see visions,*
> *Your old men shall dream dreams* (Joel 2:17).

And, just as the 120 waited in the upper room in Jerusalem for the Promise of the Father, let us be joyful and expectant as we, too, wait for this final move of the Holy Spirit. Be glad and rejoice when the Holy Spirit falls on ALL flesh – not just on believers but on those who once rejected Christ. And be prepared for surprises. Just as Pentecost led to the Gentiles coming into the kingdom faster than the Jews, so, too, the ones who were once steeped in sin have been born again through the prayers of the saints. You prayed them in.

Hallelujah! Rejoice that new babes in Christ are prophesying and having dreams and visions. For God is no respecter of persons. Whether seasoned warriors or new believers we are all called to bring in the end-time harvest.

Those who are still on earth at the start of the tribulation will all be sealed for service unto the Lord.

> *After these things I saw four angels standing at the four corners of the earth, holding the four winds of the earth, that the wind should not blow on the earth, on the sea, or on any tree. Then I saw another angel ascending from the east, having the seal of the living God. And he cried with a loud voice to the four angels to whom it was granted to harm the earth and the sea, saying, "Do not harm the earth, the sea, or the trees till we have sealed the servants of our God on their foreheads." And I heard the number of those who were sealed. One hundred and forty-four thousand of all the tribes of the children of Israel were sealed* (Revelation 7:1-4).

The ones who are sealed total 144,000 and come from the twelve tribes of Israel. But I do not think it should be taken literally. The twelve tribes are representative of all new covenant believers. 144 comprises 12 x 12, and 12 denotes completion. Therefore the total number of 144,000 signifies multiples of 12 and covers an unlimited number of servants who will complete their final assignment. It covers all of God's covenant people who have not embraced the mark of the beast and who will take the gospel to the four corners of the earth.

Are you glad to be counted as God's faithful servant? Then join me in giving thanks to the Lord Most High for giving us the Holy Spirit to equip us for our mission.

Acknowledgments

I'd like to take this opportunity to express my gratitude to and to honor all the people in my life that have been a great blessing to me. All of you have provided support and stood by me through this process. I wish to thank you for your contributions to my inspiration and knowledge, and let you know how much I appreciate your help with this book.

First and foremost, I'd like to honor my husband Apostle Gregory McCurry for his pure love, sympathetic guidance and compassionate heart for the people of God. I am forever grateful that you are a part of my life. You are my best friend, my Pastor, my Confidant and my Ride or Die. I love you to life and there is nothing you can do about it!!!

To Fleur Vaz, all the way from Malaysia, my content editor, thank you for helping me organize this project, restructure the content and stay on track. I could not have done it without you. I know without a doubt the Holy Spirit guided me straight to you. I know we will work together on future projects. Blessings, my Friend. Pastor Denise Washington my **"Girl Friday"** I appreciate you and all you do. Sis Adrianne Kincaid for transcribing all my sermons from the series.

My spiritual mentor, Apostle Winnie E. Hamilton, the mother to the nations. Apostle Hamilton, I'm so grateful for your advice, prayers, and "more homework than was humanly possible to be completed in this lifetime." I love the God in you that brings out the God in me. You encourage me to seek newer and deeper places in God and a greater level of growth in His glory and power. **I AM A PROPHET TO**

THE NATIONS!! I accept all the calling of God for me.

To my bonus daughter, Sonja McCurry, "the minister of Music t." I thank God for your YES!! I see you much growth in you " When I think about you future I have to put on sunglasses IT IS BRIGTH!!" And my Salon Team at Ulta Beauty Mayfield ... much love ladies! Teamwork makes the dream work.

I'd like to thank all of my New Beginning Ministries family for your service to the body of Christ. To the new Beginnanites are the BEST!! Chief – Apostle Leon and Senior Pastor Margie Nelson – our ministry covering – thank you for your daily prayers. I have learned so much from watching how you conduct yourselves in your personal lives and from your integrity.

My sincere thanks as well to the following individuals, without whose contribution and support, this book would not have been written: Kingdom Kidz Ministry – I LOVE MY BABIES, My Mentor Mom and Dad, Alvin and Helen Copeland for your unconditional love and unfailing support, Mrs. Janet Tull my best friend and sister in Christ FOREVER.

Be Blessed, but most of all Be Inspired!

~ Teresa S. McCurry, CIO, Inspire Me Inc. & Senior Pastor, New Beginning Ministries

Invest in you!! Hire Teresa as your Beauty Entrepreneur,

Coach, and Ministry Leader

She Can Really Make a Difference!

Through her Impact as an educator, Teresa quickly discovered her ability to inspire fellow Beauty Entrepreneurs and Ministry Leaders. Those formulas, processes and "Inspirational Recipes" that she has developed could also help other Beauty Entrepreneurs and Ministry Leaders grow their businesses and leadership teams.

Most importantly, she realized that she could help Beauty Entrepreneur coaches and Ministry Leaders achieve success more quickly with fewer challenges by teaching them what took her years to develop through her own trial and error experiences in business and ministry.

Whether you are just starting a business or ministry, if you're well into your venture, the idea of hiring a business/Ministry coach may have come to mind. But you may be wondering if a business/Ministry coach can really make a difference for you. To answer this, you need to understand what a business/ Ministry coach does, and how to choose the right one.

An effective Beauty Entrepreneur coach and Ministry Leadership trainer will help you determine, not just the direction you want for your business or ministry, but will also identify actionable steps by implementing a strategic plan of action to achieve the goals you and your coach set....

Call Teresa for a $30/30-minute "Inspiration Consultation"

"Coaching is unlocking a person's potential to maximize their own performance. It is helping them to learn rather than teaching them…"

-John Whitmore

I HAVE BEEN COACHING

Since 2006, I have been blessed to coach Beauty Entrepreneurs, Small Business owners, Ministry leaders and purpose-driven individuals go to the next Level by uniquely helping them experience their God-given purpose and find freedom from what is holding them back.

I would be thrilled to offer you a $30/30 minute, "Inspiration Consultation" to see if we are a fit for each other … either by phone, by Skype or in person (if geographically possible!) If you're open, the best way to get in touch would be to FB message me or just fill out the contact form on the my website www.InspireMeInc.com

Be blessed, but most of all Be Inspired!!!

Teresa S. McCurry, CIO - Chief Inspirational Officer, Inspire Me Inc.

Senior Pastor, New Beginning Ministries

McCurry Ministries International

Appendix & Resources

http://www.enhancemyvocabulary.com

https://www.blueletterbible.org

https://www.biblegateway.com

www.gotquestions.org

About the author

Senior Pastor Teresa McCurry is an ordained minister of the Gospel of Jesus Christ. She co-labors with her husband, Apostle Gregory McCurry, of New Beginning Ministries doing the work of the Lord as a ministry team.

"We introduce a Real God, to Real people with Real issues"

Pastor Tee was called to ministry in 2010 under the leadership of Apostle Leon and Pastor Margie Nelson. She has traveled extensively, educating and inspiring others with her unique approach of conveying information. She has a heart for doing missions work around the world.

This was the beginnings of a great and powerful deliverance move of God in her life to reach the hurting and lost. God anointed Pastor Tee with spiritual eyesight and ability to speak into people's lives and immediately deliverance takes place to bring forth healing to broken-hearted souls, to proclaim liberty to the captives, and set their hearts completely free.

Pastor Tee is dedicated to helping people who seek to make a positive change.

Her marketplace ministry extends beyond the walls of the church. She is a Beauty Entrepreneur Coach, Inspirational Speaker, Author of the book *Runnin' Things: The Resilient Spirit of an Entrepreneur*, and a licensed cosmetologist with over 30 years of beauty industry experience. She holds a Bachelor's degree in Applied Business Administration.

She is currently the President & CIO of Inspire Me Incorporated, Salon Manager at The Salon at ULTA Beauty and, she Chairs Christian Networking Entrepreneurs "CNE" an community outreach of NBM. We encourage creative thinking, inspire meaningful dialogue and promote personal and business development through fellowship that will spotlight and support Christian businesses.

She is the founder of The MCS~Fund whose sole mission to generate unrestricted funds for Sickle Cell Anemia affected individuals. Through Supportive Services & Advocacy, serving the needs of people plagued by this disease is not only a mission, but a passion.

Pastor Tee also serves on the Board of Directors at Detroit Shoreway Community Development Organization (DSCDO), as an Institutional Representative.

Invest in you !!

Inspirational Speaking

Teresa brings her knowledge, research and business savvy to audiences as a keynote speaker. Teresa's inspirational and transformational programs are filled with actionable takeaways. Let Teresa bring this energy to your next event!

Leadership Enhancement

Teresa can help you develop the necessary resources and competencies to become an effective leader in any situation. Her seminars provide various avenues for improving the qualities of good leadership in you and in your team.

- Beauty Entrepreneurship Coach
- International Keynote Speaker
- Ministry Leadership Trainer
- International Bible Teacher

Teresa shares how leaders Inspire, Influence and Realize results.

~Women's Day ~International Keynote ~ Panelist ~

~Mistress of Ceremony ~ Workshop Facilitator

Teresa is available for speaking engagements, workshops & seminars;

Contact her at:
Teresa@InspireMeInc.com
Info@mynewbeginning.org
(216) 916-9270 ext. 4
www.MyNewBeginning.org,
New Beginning Ministries
2060 west 65th Street
Cleveland, Ohio 44102

Follow her on social media

#RunninThings, #InspireMeSuperTee, #McCurryMinistriesInt

Face book:

Teresa S. Mccurry

Inspire Me Inc.

Beauty Entrepreneurs Networking B.E.N.

Christian Networking Entrepreneurs

Twitter:

@inspiremesuper

Instagram:

inspiremesupert

Linked in:

Teresa S. McCurry

YouTube:

Pastor Teresa McCurry

LeTonya F. Moore, JD is an attorney-entrepreneur with almost twenty years of experience building and helping build successful enterprises. She is the visionary behind 360° Brand Protection Strategies™, developed to address the holistic needs of the entrepreneur. The 360° methodology enables brands to develop strategic growth and expansion to the national, international, and global marketplace. Recently, LeTonya reached a major milestone of introducing her brand protection methodology to the United Kingdom in 2018. She is the founding member of The Global Growth Group (G3), a society of experts collaborating to provide entrepreneurs, including speakers, authors, and coaches with a guided pathway to global protecting their brand both in the US and abroad. Through her work, she is now affectionately known as the Global Brand Protector ™

LeTonya is a sought after speaker who brings value and shares priceless insight and wisdom with her audiences. LeTonya is no stranger to overcoming obstacles and living life on purpose, with purpose. She shares her success story in her, "LeTonya Speaks" motivational presentations that spread a message of faith, perseverance, and the hard work to audiences small and large. LeTonya's "Real Talk" presentation style proves enlightening, educational, and entertaining for diverse demographics.

SPEAKING TOPICS
1. BRAND PROTECTION: LOOKING BEYOND PATENTS, TRADEMARKS, & COPYRIGHTS
2. BUILDING A B.A.I.L. TEAM: PROTECTING YOUR $, YOUR BOOKS, YOUR ASSETS, & YOUR LEGACY
3. 6 M's of BRAND PROTECTION: MINDEST, MOTIVATION, MONIKER, MONEY, MARKETING, & MASTERY
4. HOW TO STOP BRAND STEALING THIEVES WITH A BRAND PROTECTION PLAYBOOK
5. THE TRAILBLAZEHER ™: MY JOURNEY FROM TEEN MOM TO GLOBAL BRAND PROTECTOR

To learn more about LeTonya Moore visit her official website at www.letonyamoore.com.
Follow her on Facebook @iprotectyourbrand
Follow her on Twitter/IG/Snapchat/LinkedIn @letonyamoore
Direct Dial: 256-472-2631 Schedule Consult

TERESA S. MCCURRY

THE PERSON WITH POWER

The Agent-Owned Cloud Brokerage®

Let Pamela help you make your realty dreams a reality!

*Buying   *Selling   *First-Time Buyer   *Investor   *Relocation   *Career

Pamela is a licensed REALTOR® in the Commonwealth of Virginia

Not in Virginia? No Problem

We're in all fifty states; I can connect you with an agent who services your area.   Call me , visit my website, or like me on Face Book.

Interested in a career in real estate? To explore a career with Exp Realty Go to:

http://pamelawestbrook.exprealty.careers/

Pamela Westbrook

Broker/**REALTOR**®

(866) 825-7169 Ext. 456

Email: Pamela.westbrook@exprealty.com

Website: pamelawestbrook.exprealty.com

Facebook—www.facebook.com/pwestbrookrealestate

www.ingramcontent.com/pod-product-compliance
Lightning Source LLC
Chambersburg PA
CBHW030859170426
43193CB00009BA/674